Traditional Tapa
Textiles of the Pacific

Traditional Tapa Textiles of the Pacific

With 243 illustrations, 202 in color and 3 maps

Roger Neich and Mick Pendergrast

Photography by Krzysztof Pfeiffer

THAMES AND HUDSON

Page 1: Decorative motif from a Tongan tapa cloth.

Page 2: *Siapo tasina*, Samoa. The design on this tapa is the result of rubbing on an elaborate leaf *upeti*, with no further overpainting. Without a definite record of origin, it is often very difficult to determine whether sheets like this were made in Tonga or Samoa.

Title page: Tapa mask cover, Nakanai people, New Britain, Papua New Guinea. This small mask cover was used for funeral ceremonies which marked the death of an important man.

Below: A dove motif from Tonga.

First published in paperback in the United States of America in 1998
by Thames and Hudson Inc., 500 Fifth Avenue, New York, New York 10110
in association with David Bateman Ltd, 30 Tarndale Grove, Albany, Auckland, New Zealand

Copyright © 1997 David Bateman Ltd, Auckland

ISBN 0-500-27989-6

Library of Congress Catalog Card Number 97-61529

Printed and bound in Hong Kong by Colorcraft Ltd

CONTENTS

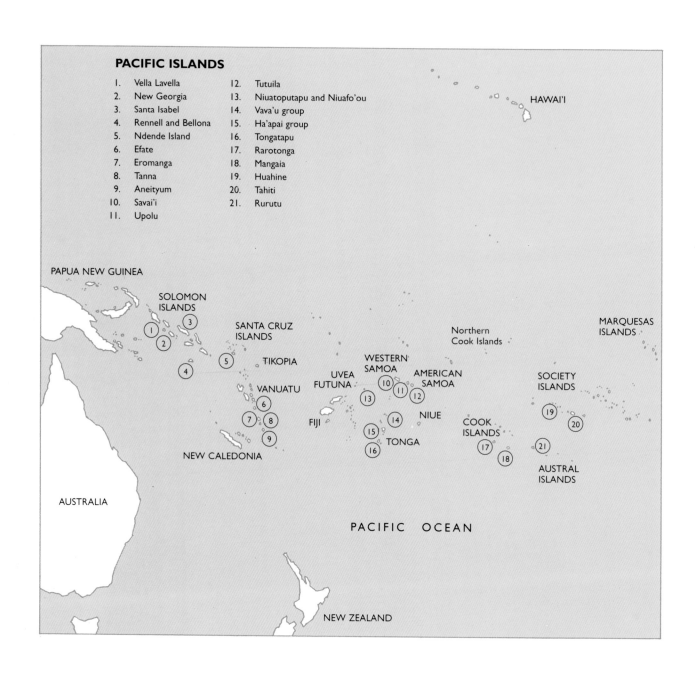

PACIFIC ISLANDS

1. Vella Lavella
2. New Georgia
3. Santa Isabel
4. Rennell and Bellona
5. Ndende Island
6. Efate
7. Eromanga
8. Tanna
9. Aneityum
10. Savai'i
11. Upolu
12. Tutuila
13. Niuatoputapu and Niuafo'ou
14. Vava'u group
15. Ha'apai group
16. Tongatapu
17. Rarotonga
18. Mangaia
19. Huahine
20. Tahiti
21. Rurutu

HAWAI'I

PAPUA NEW GUINEA

SOLOMON
ISLANDS

SANTA CRUZ
ISLANDS

MARQUESAS
ISLANDS

TIKOPIA

Northern
Cook Islands

VANUATU

UVEA
FUTUNA

WESTERN
SAMOA

AMERICAN
SAMOA

SOCIETY
ISLANDS

FIJI

NIUE

COOK
ISLANDS

NEW CALEDONIA

TONGA

AUSTRAL
ISLANDS

AUSTRALIA

PACIFIC   OCEAN

NEW ZEALAND

Preceding pages: *Siapo mamanu*, Samoa.
Collected in Fiji, this freehand painted
pattern of stylized leaves is probably of
Samoan origin. 143 × 184 cm.

CHAPTER 1

TAPA IN THE PACIFIC

Tapa or barkcloth made from the inner bark of certain trees, especially the paper mulberry, is one of the most distinctive products of the cultures of the Pacific islands. Some of the peoples of South America, Africa, South-East Asia, the Philippines and Indonesia also made tapa, but it probably reached its greatest refinement and variety among the islands of the South Pacific. Even the name "tapa", which is now used worldwide for barkcloth, had its origins in Polynesia during the early nineteenth-century years of European contact. The word is derived from the Samoan word *tapa* for the uncoloured border of a barkcloth sheet and the Hawaiian *kapa* for a variety of barkcloth. In several parts of Melanesia, from New Guinea to Vanuatu, in Fiji, and on most of the high islands of Polynesia from Hawaii in the north to Tahiti, the Marquesas, Tonga, Samoa, Niue, the Cook Islands and even New Zealand, the manufacture of barkcloth is an ancient craft which has been practised for thousands of years. In many of these areas where the craft flourished, it became a major vehicle for women's creative expression. In some parts of New Guinea, in the Marquesas Islands and in Easter Island, men also made tapa, especially for use on ritual objects such as masks, figures and loincloths.

Barkcloth around the world may be made from several different plants but in the Pacific islands the most commonly used plant is the paper mulberry (*Broussonetia papyrifera*). The early peoples who populated the Pacific brought cuttings of this plant, which was originally a native of eastern Asia, with them in their canoes. In the tropical Pacific, the paper mulberry plant does not flower or set seed, so it has to be propagated from cuttings or suckers and is cultivated specifically for tapa-making. Another source of barkcloth in the Pacific is the breadfruit (*Artocarpus*), grown mainly for its fruit which is a staple food in many islands. The use of its bark for tapa is only secondary. Bark from various species of banyan or wild fig (*Ficus*) also provides a heavier type of tapa in some parts of the Pacific.

The skill and knowledge of making cloth from bark, and even some of the necessary plants, were carried out of South-East Asia by the first peoples to move into the South Pacific islands. Some archaeological evidence suggests that tapa was being made in southern China and mainland South-East Asia more than five thousand years ago. From there, the craft spread into eastern Indonesia where the techniques were developed and refined over some thousands of years. Barkcloth made by the Toradja people of central Sulawesi still shares many of the techniques and artistic motifs found thousands of kilometres eastward in Polynesia.

Most of the linguistic and archaeological evidence supports the theory that tapa-making was one of the ancient skills that the Lapita ancestors of the Polynesians brought with them about three thousand years ago, down through the islands of Melanesia and out into the wider Pacific. Named after their distinctive patterned pottery, the Lapita people possibly used similar designs in their body tattoo and on their barkcloth. Art experts have argued that these designs and their incorporation into larger patterns can still be discerned on barkcloth made in Polynesia today.

The inner bark of the paper mulberry tree, *Broussonetia papyrifera,* is the basis for many of the barkcloth, tapa, products of the Pacific.

Complicating this simplified picture are the various different traditions of tapa-making among the very diverse cultures of Melanesia. Understanding how these Melanesian tapa traditions relate to each other, and to the Polynesian tapa complex, requires much further research and may never be known in detail.

Much of this prehistory can at present only be speculation, because the archaeological evidence of ancient tapa-making in the Pacific is so sparse. For Polynesia, the earliest evidence is a series of seven wooden barkcloth beaters found in the waterlogged occupation site of Vaito'otia and Fa'ahia on Huahine in the Society Islands, dating from the ninth to the thirteenth centuries AD. After this, the only other pre-European material evidence of Polynesian tapa-making is the New Zealand Maori barkcloth beater found near the sixteenth- or seventeenth-century *pa* on Lake Mangakaware in the Waikato. Several other early but undated tapa beaters have been found in the swamps and tidal estuaries of northern New Zealand. Despite this lack of material evidence, Pacific tapa is clearly the result of a continuous development spanning many centuries. About two hundred years ago, when European travellers reached the Pacific islands, they began to assemble the amazing collections of tapa cloth that continue to delight and inspire us today.

Even while Pacific cultures changed and responded to the impact and challenge of European intervention, village women in many areas continued to produce tapa cloth, adapting and innovating to suit the new conditions. Some techniques were streamlined, new tools were utilised, introduced dyes and foreign motifs were incorporated into the work, and the finished product was sometimes made up into new types of clothing, but the basic craft persisted. European travellers and, soon, interested tourists, encouraged this continuing production of women's art which often survives – even when the special artistic expressions of village men in carving or canoe-building or mask-making have been overtaken by the products of the

A Samoan girl in a photographer's studio, in Apia, Western Samoa. Late nineteenth-century studio photographers working in Fiji and Samoa kept sheets of tapa cloth for use as props. Consequently, the same sheet often appears in several different photographs.

industrial world. Consequently, museum collections of tapa provide a panorama of changing techniques and styles through the nineteenth and early twentieth centuries.

Within each culture that produces and uses it, tapa serves a wide range of purposes, both utilitarian and ceremonial. For many of these cultures, clothing – or at least coverings for basic modesty such as loincloths and G-strings – is the main use of tapa. But even at this common everyday level, in some cultures, such as the Orokaiva of the Musa River in Papua New Guinea, the patterns on tapa clothing also convey signals about clan allegiance. On a wider scale, where large cultures met and traded in the past, such as in the Tonga-Fiji-Samoa region, patterns on barkcloth immediately identified their source. Other Pacific cultures reserve barkcloth for ceremonial and ritual purposes; presenting it to honoured guests, wearing special tapa clothing for festivals, making masks of tapa to parade the spirits through the villages, using tapa to wrap the images of their gods, and even to make images of the gods themselves.

With such a huge variety of tapa patterns and functions in evidence, it is no surprise that the first Europeans who arrived in the Pacific soon came to regard tapa cloth as one of the most obvious symbols of a Pacific identity. Tapa could also be conveniently cut up into small pieces to take back to Europe as distinctive souvenirs of Pacific travels. As early as 1787, Alexander Shaw published a little booklet of tapa samples collected on Captain Cook's Pacific voyages, with descriptions of the manufacturing process. Nineteenth-century photographers working in the Pacific frequently used sheets of tapa cloth as props and clothing for their models, helping to establish patterned tapa as an easily recognized symbol of the exotic Pacific. Nowadays, for many Pacific Island people themselves living in the large metropolitan centres around the Pacific Rim, traditional tapa designs printed on cotton cloth, or applied to plastics, have become a marker of their special identity in a grey industrial world.

Tapa manufacture by Toto'a Fagai, 1980, Vaito'omuli, Savai'i, Western Samoa.
(a) Toto'a bites around the bark of a paper mulberry sapling to free the bark for stripping.
(b) The soft inner bark or bast is pulled away from the stiff outer bark.
(c) Toto'a scrapes the bast on a sloping board with a seashell to remove any outer bark remnants.
(d) Beating the bast on the *tutua* or wooden anvil.
(e) A strip of bast after beating is completed.
(f) Rubbing the sheet on a wooden *upeti* with an arrowroot tuber. The pattern gradually
emerges on the tapa cloth.
(g) Lifting the tapa from the *upeti* with the pattern imprinted on to the cloth where it was touching the
board, leaving the grooves uncoloured.

CHAPTER 2

MAKING TAPA

The various techniques of barkcloth manufacture practised in the Pacific are all variations on a central theme. This method commences by stripping the bark from the tree, separating the inner from the outer bark – which is discarded – and then beating the inner bark on an anvil, usually with wooden beaters, to spread the fibres. Where beaters with different gauges of grooving are used, beating begins with the coarsest grooves and progresses to the finest grooves, sometimes to a smooth-surfaced beater or a patterned beater for the final effect. Water may or may not be introduced at certain stages of this process, and in some cases soaking, or even a degree of fermenting, is allowed to soften and macerate the fibres. To produce larger pieces, thin sheets can be layered and felted together during beating, gradually extending the size of the finished sheet. This felting technique was more characteristic of tapa made in the islands of eastern Polynesia, whereas in western Polynesia larger runs of tapa were usually made by pasting sheets together at their edges. Throughout the Pacific islands, much wider variation developed among the different techniques employed for applying colour and designs to this cloth. Some of these colouring and patterning techniques were carried out as part of the sheet-making process, while others were applied to the completed plain sheet.

Within each of the tapa-making cultures of the Pacific, this central theme has been developed in different ways, resulting in various sets of techniques which are specific to each culture. It is these sets of techniques which produce such distinctive tapa cloth from the different islands of the Pacific. No single detailed description of the beating, layering and colouring methods involved in tapa-making can do justice to the special nature of the manufacturing process followed in each culture. To give some idea of the complexity of the process and the finely tuned skills required, the manufacture of tapa cloth as followed in Samoa will serve as an example.

In Samoan villages, small plantations of paper mulberry trees, known here as *u'a*, are grown near the houses for the manufacture of tapa cloth. The inner bark of breadfruit and banyan trees was also used for making tapa, but only the paper mulberry is specially planted for this purpose. For ten to fourteen months, the plants are tended carefully to ensure they grow straight without branches which would cause holes and scars in the finished cloth. When they are ready, a straight sapling about 1 metre (3 feet) long and 5 cm (2 in) in diameter is cut. Then the worker cuts or bites around the sapling so that the bark can be stripped from the stick by a strong, even pull. This bark strip is rolled up inside out and a knife is then used to start separating the soft pliable inner bark, or bast, from the coarse outer layer which is discarded. Next, the bast is laid on a sloping board, kept constantly wet, and scraped with a sea shell to clean away any remnants of bark. This scraping also softens and spreads the fibres. In earlier times, the scraping process was carried out while sitting in a stream as a ready source of water. But women found this cold, uncomfortable work and the shell scrapers were hard on their hands. More recently, the scraping is done inside a house with a basin of water nearby. Sometimes now, when large

Left: Toto'a overpainting the imprinted design with elaborated freehand additions. Her 'o'a dye is held in an old corned beef tin beside her and she uses a pandanus fruit as a paintbrush.

Opposite: Designs carved on both sides of the *upeti* owned by Toto'a. For economy, many modern flat wooden *upeti* have a different design carved on each side, as on this *upeti*, carved by her husband Fagai.

Opposite below: Two *siapo vala* made by Toto'a and her helpers. These show the wide range of final designs that have been produced by individual freehand overpainting on patterns imprinted from the *upeti* shown above.

amounts of *siapo* (Samoan for tapa) are needed in short order for a special occasion, the scraping process is omitted entirely. Scraping does produce a very fine, clean, white *siapo* without any brown traces of outer bark remaining. Direct beating, without scraping, does not give such fine white cloth but it is much quicker and easier, and for most modern purposes of exchange and sale to tourists, it produces *siapo* of satisfactory quality.

To thin and spread the bast to form cloth, the next step is to beat it on a wooden anvil or *tutua* with wooden beaters called *i'e*. In earlier times, about ten pieces would be beaten at the same time, folded according to a definite pattern. Nowadays, only two or three pieces might be processed together, and sometimes only one at a time. Working to a definite sequence and rhythm, beating commences with a wide-grooved beater facet and progresses to a smooth side for the final beating, when cloth of the desired width and thickness has been produced. At the completion of the beating process, the bundle is set on edge on the anvil and struck with two or three deliberate strokes of the smooth side of the beater. After beating, the individual sheets are separated and stretched out on the mats in the house or outside on the grass and weighted down with stones to dry.

Natural dyes for colouring these sheets of white tapa are obtained from various trees and plants. Juice from the bark of the *'o'a* tree (*Bischofia javanica*) provides a reddish-brown colour which can also be mixed with other dyes. From the bark of the *lama* or candlenut tree (*Aleurites moluccana*) comes another brown dye; burning the nuts of this tree gives off a soot that is used as a black dye. Yellow colouring comes from the roots of the turmeric plant (*Curcuma longa*) and was a favourite colour on early freehand painted *siapo*, but on old sheets it has often faded completely away. A bright red dye called *loa* is obtained from the seeds of *Bixa orellana* which was introduced into Samoa early last century. Red ochre called *'ele* is spread as grated powder over the barkcloth surface, then rubbed into the fibres with a pad dipped in *'o'a* juice. The sources of *'ele* are limited to certain localities on Tutuila and Upolu, so lumps of the ochre were traded widely across the Samoan islands.

For decorating *siapo*, Samoans have two alternative techniques which are usually applied exclusively on a particular sheet. In the simplest technique, patterns are painted on freehand to create *siapo mamanu*. This method gives full rein to women's

creativity, but a range of recognized motifs has developed as a basic design vocabulary. Some are very ancient motifs that can be traced back into Indonesia, but others are recent innovations. Many of these motifs are given descriptive names drawn from the natural world, such as breadfruit leaves, pandanus leaves, pandanus bloom, fishnet, trochus shell, starfish, worm, centipede, and footprints of various birds. Through all

the years of *siapo* production in Samoa, women have exercised their artistic freedom in the combination of these motifs so that virtually every *siapo mamanu* is unique in its design. Period lettering, spelling out names of people and places, has also been incorporated into some of these designs.

In a more complex technique, the patterns are transferred on to the white tapa from design tablets to produce repeating patterned tapa called *siapo tasina* or *siapo 'elei* – after the name of the rubbing process which involves *'ele* red ochre. In earlier times, Samoan design tablets, known as *upeti*, were made by sewing pieces of coconut midrib, bamboo strips and sennit in patterns on to a rectangle of pandanus leaves. This tablet was then tied to a board, or often a piece of an old dugout canoe, to hold it rigid for the rubbing process. Leaf *upeti* were still being used until about the 1920s, by which time they were gradually replaced by wooden carved *upeti*. The idea of wooden carved *upeti* may have been introduced into Samoa from Fiji where they were used at an early date. Designs are carved on both sides of modern flat wooden *upeti* and, being much more durable and convenient to use, it is no wonder that the old intricate leaf *upeti* were abandoned. Old leaf *upeti* produced very fine intricate imprints, with every detail of the stitched patterns showing through – readily distinguished from the bolder blocks of colour on design imprints resulting from a wooden *upeti*.

This change from leaf *upeti* to wooden *upeti* also brought about a gender change in the production of Samoan *siapo* design. Leaf *upeti* were made by women, and hence they were responsible for the composition of their designs. With the introduction of wooden carved tablets, men – frequently the husbands of the tapa-makers – became the designers. Since the change in *upeti* types, basic *siapo* design has also changed from being women's art to men's art. However, the change is not as drastic as it may seem. The male designers have clearly preserved the basic features of earlier *siapo* design as developed by women leaf tablet artists. Furthermore, the designs on later wooden *upeti* are quite rudimentary, leaving plenty of scope for the woman doing the final freehand overpainting of the imprinted design to exercise her own imagination in emphasizing different aspects of the basic design. This freedom means that a wide range of final *siapo* designs can be produced from a very limited set of *upeti* patterns. Women often lend their wooden *upeti* to other tapa makers, spreading their basic designs wider and introducing even more variation into the final product.

In the rubbing process, the plain sheet of tapa is laid over the tablet then rubbed with a pad of old tapa that is continually dipped in *'o'a* dye. This transfers the pattern through the tapa where it is in contact with the tablet, leaving the pattern showing on both sides of the cloth. Usually at this stage of the process, the patching of holes, the glueing together of sheets, and the design imprinting are all done simultaneously on the *upeti*. The glue for patching and sticking the sheets together is a starchy arrowroot tuber called *masoa* which is rubbed over the joins as extra sheets are laid in on the *upeti*. Interspersed with the patching and glueing, more *'o'a* dye is rubbed in, along with powdered red ochre *'ele*, which is grated in a thin spread over the cloth. Each time the cloth is moved one register across the *upeti*, another repeat of the design is produced, usually about four to eight times for a modern *siapo vala*. On large middle to late nineteenth-century *siapo tasina*, the *upeti* pattern is repeated many times to cover the full size of the sheet. Many of these large sheets from last century were finished at this stage, without any freehand highlighting. For smaller sheets, freehand overpainting with the same dyes to emphasize selected aspects of the design complete the tapa, which was then laid out to dry.

Opposite: A selection of *siapo vala* by Toto'a and her helpers also based on the *upeti* shown on page 15.

SAMOA

Opposite: *Siapo mamanu,*
Samoa. Recorded as being
collected in Fiji, this tapa
displays the heavy brownish-
black resinous glaze typical of
Samoan tapa painted with *'o'a*
sap mixed with special charcoal,
or black dye, from *lama* nut
kernels. 208 × 167 cm.

On the high fertile volcanic islands of Savai'i, Upolu, Tutuila, and the Manu'a Islands in the heart of western Polynesia, live the Samoans who form the most populous branch of the tropical Polynesian people. Despite the modern political division into Western Samoa and American Samoa, Samoan culture and language are virtually the same throughout the archipelago.

Strong links of kinship, indigenous political alliances and religion – both ancient and Christian – have always bound all the Samoan people together. While many different varieties of tapa or *siapo* have been made in Samoa, homogeneity of Samoan culture is generally reflected in the widespread distribution of these *siapo* varieties and the absence of strong regional differences in types and decorative motifs. This contrasts with Fiji, for example, where linguistic and cultural differences within the archipelago are also expressed in the development of different regional forms of tapa.

According to some early accounts, the wearing of *siapo* as an item of clothing in old Samoa was restricted to a privileged few unmarried women of the highest status who only wore it about the houses. Then this rule gradually broke down as men and women of any rank began to wear tapa as part of their ordinary and ceremonial dress. Barkcloth was worn as a *lavalava* by men and women, wrapped around men's heads like a turban, as a loincloth or girdle by men, and in strips as a belt (*fusi*) over fine mats or other sheets of *siapo* in the ceremonial dress of the *manaia* (leader of the young men of the village) and *taupou* (village virgin). Early European missionaries soon introduced the Tahitian-style barkcloth poncho or *tiputa* to encourage women to cover their upper bodies in keeping with missionary ideas of modesty. Photographs from the later nineteenth century show orators wearing *siapo vala* as *lavalava*, and women with tapa clothing often made up into blouses or full dresses.

Orator chiefs, c.1930s, Western Samoa. Standing in traditional pose with their flywhisks and *to'oto'o* staff as attributes of office, the talking chiefs at left and right wear *siapo vala* as *lavalava*, wrap-around skirts, while the central chief wears a plaited *'ie toga* held by a tapa belt.

Above left: Orator chief and family, 1890s, Palauli, Savai'i, Western Samoa. The older man in a naval jacket and cotton *lavalava* holds a flywhisk or *fue* as a mark of his office as a talking chief. The younger man wears a freehand painted *siapo lavalava* held in place by a tapa cloth belt.

Above right: Young men dressed as *manaia*, c. 1900s, Apia, Western Samoa. Holding their *nifo'oti* weapons and wearing *siapo lavalava* with full ceremonial *tuiga* headdress, these young chiefs' sons are prepared for their role as *manaia*, when they will perform the same duties normally carried out by the *taupou*.

Left: Young women in tapa dresses, c. 1900s, Apia, Western Samoa. These outfits have been cut and shaped in European-style from freehand painted *siapo*.

Imported cloth soon replaced *siapo* as an article of general clothing, but it continued to be worn for special occasions.

Apart from its use in clothing, large sheets of *siapo* served as curtains (*pupuni*) for dividing up the space of large open guest houses, as bed covers, and as mosquito nets (*ta'i namu*). Before the introduction of coffins, a body was wrapped in a large *siapo* burial shroud. In most of these instances today, imported materials have replaced tapa. For a wedding in a Samoan church, tapa is laid along the aisle, but since Samoans have given up making large lengths of tapa cloth, Tongan tapa is now imported for

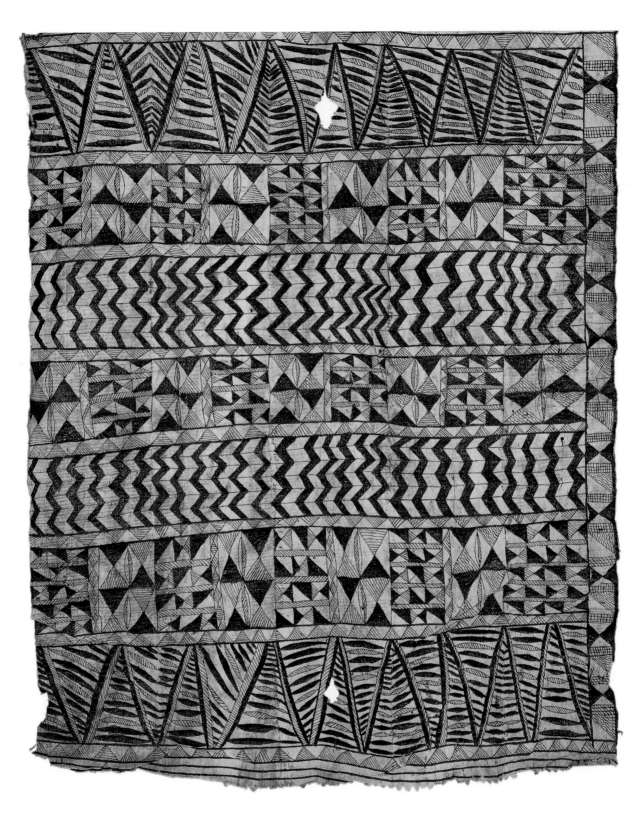

Siapo mamanu, Samoa.
231 × 186 cm.

this purpose. Another modern use is for tablecloths, accounting for many of the circular sheets of tapa seen in twentieth-century collections.

Throughout Samoan history, *siapo* has maintained its major role as an item of exchange and formal presentation. At all Samoan special occasions such as births, funerals, weddings, and investiture of *matai* titles, sheets of tapa are included in the presentations and exchanges of valuables between families that accompany these ceremonies. Part of the payment to expert house and canoe builders consisted of *siapo*. In the formal presentations of gifts to special visitors or honoured guests, such

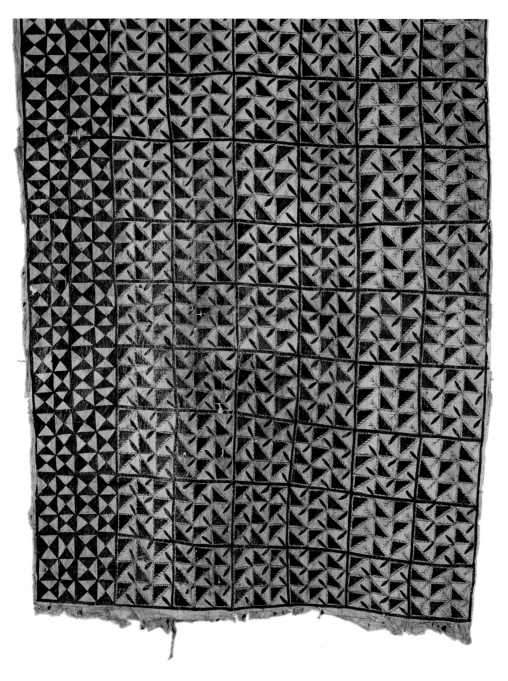

as the *sua ta'i* and the *ta'alolo* gift procession, sheets of *siapo* always had a special place. In the Samoan economic system, *i'e toga* or fine mats are the most prestigious of Samoan valuables, followed by *siapo*. But during the New Zealand Administration's attempt to suppress the Mau independence movement in Western Samoa in the 1920s, the presentation of fine mats was prohibited. This led to the substitution of many sheets of *siapo* at weddings, funerals and political meetings. In more modern times, *siapo* has tended to pass out of use on these occasions, as the elaboration of many new kinds of decorated plaited mats has developed.

Both before and after European contact, Samoan styles of tapa have been introduced to other parts of the Pacific. For centuries, inter-island trade had moved specialised items such as red parakeet feathers for decorating fine mats, tapa, sandalwood, whales' teeth, and canoes between Fiji, Tonga and Samoa. Tapa techniques and designs also followed these routes of exchange. In the late eighteenth century, Samoan canoe builders of the Lemaki clan from Manono settled in the Lau Islands of Fiji under Tongan protection. Along with their wives, they may have been

Siapo mamanu, Samoa. In this freehand painted design, the artist has emphasized the triangular pattern by the addition of yellow turmeric. 160 × 146 cm.

responsible for the presence of some Samoan tapa styles in Lau. On Niue, the influence of Christian Samoan missionaries and their wives was so strong that much of the tapa collected in Niue during the later nineteenth century is identical to Samoan *siapo*. Samoan missionary families who served in New Britain and New Ireland in the Bismarck Archipelago and around the coasts of Papua at the turn of the century and later, probably carried sheets of *siapo* with them for their own use. They even perhaps shared some of their tapa-making skills with the local people – in the same way that they often taught Samoan basketry and mat-plaiting techniques to their host Papuan communities. As a result of this movement and exchange of motifs, techniques and actual pieces of tapa cloth, large nineteenth-century collections often contain pieces of tapa whose origin is now very difficult to distinguish.

A modern exception to the wide geographical spread of Samoan tapa motifs and designs throughout the Samoan archipelago is the distinctive style of freehand painted *siapo* which developed in Leone village on Tutuila during the 1920s, until the

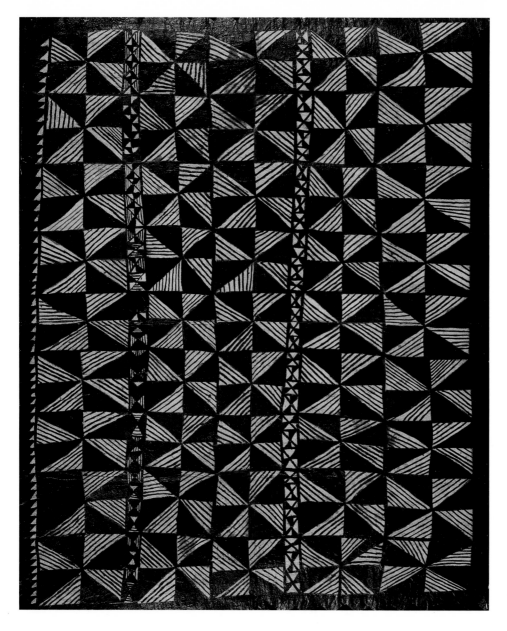

Siapo mamanu, Samoa.
A freehand painted design with
the so-called "vane swastika"
effect which is actually a very
ancient widespread pattern
used also by the Toradja people
of Indonesia. 174 x 132 cm.

A young woman dressed as a
taupou, c. 1900s, Apia, Western
Samoa. In the full costume of a
village virgin, or taupou, with
her tuiga headdress and skirt of
fine plaited 'ie toga held up by a
tapa belt, this young daughter
of a chief is dressed to perform
the opening or closing dance
for her village or district. She is
also the person who mixes the
kava drink for an important
kava ceremony, and leads the
ta'alolo gift procession, dressed
in this outfit.

restrictions of World War II halted production. Especially under the direction of a
local Leone woman, Kolone Fai'ivae Leoso, new, bold, brightly coloured, often
circular designs, featuring motifs named after pandanus and breadfruit leaves were
frequently used in compositions often directly inspired by the stained glass windows
of the Leone Congregational Christian Church. Mary Pritchard, an American
Samoan from Pago Pago, learnt to make *siapo* from the women of Leone in the late
1920s, and through her efforts as a teacher and entrepreneur, this Leone-style of *siapo*
has now become accepted as virtually the typical tapa of American Samoa. Some rare
examples of Leone style *siapo* are still found among families in Western Samoa, but
they are probably traded heirlooms and do not seem to have influenced local Western
Samoan *siapo* design.

During the nineteenth and into the twentieth century, Samoan tapa has
undergone many changes in processes of manufacture, in decorative techniques and
motifs, and in the uses for which it has been made. Knowledge of these changes can
sometimes help to date individual pieces of Samoan tapa, thus building up a picture
of changing styles. Freehand painted tapa was very popular in Samoa in the later years
of the nineteenth century and into the 1920s when it was more common than *siapo*
dyed by rubbing on a design tablet. By the 1970s in Western Samoa, freehand *siapo*
had almost disappeared and very little was seen in circulation. *Lavalava*-sized sheets

Siapo mamanu, Samoa.
A freehand painted pattern in which the basic symmetry is relieved by many interesting variations of design and colour. 230 × 199 cm.

of *siapo vala* decorated by the *'elei* rubbing process on flat wooden *upeti*, had become the main type of *siapo* produced, both for exchange amongst Samoans themselves and for sale to tourists.

Tapa displayed at an agricultural fair, c. 1930s, Apia, Western Samoa. Displayed as part of the produce of various villages at an agricultural show, most of the designs appear to be freehand painted, suggesting that *siapo mamanu* was the most popular fashion at this period.

Following pages: Samoan tapa decorative motifs.

Siapo mamanu, Samoa. Collected in Vava'u, Tonga in the 1890s, this tapa has all the characteristics of Samoan manufacture. It features the design now called *fa'a 'aveau,* or starfish, by modern Samoan tapa-makers. However, this is an ancient pattern which has South-East Asian origins. 150 × 118 cm.

Siapo mamanu, Samoa. Recorded by the collector James Edge-Partington as coming from Niue, this freehand tapa displays another version of the *fa'a 'aveau* or starfish pattern, suggesting that it came originally from Samoa, or was made by a Samoan craftswoman working in Niue. Yellow turmeric has been used to accentuate the design. 200 × 179 cm.

Opposite: *Siapo mamanu,* Samoa. 255 × 196 cm.

29

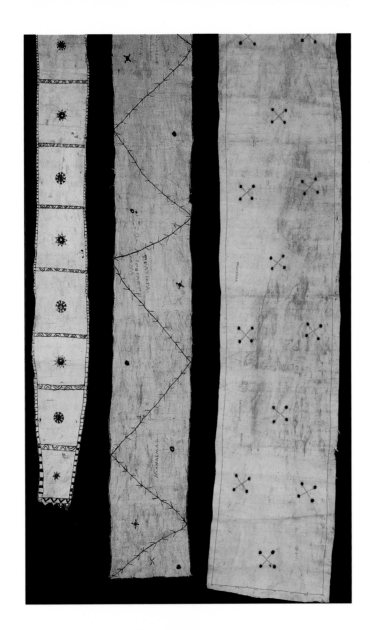

Siapo mamanu, Samoa. Old, long, narrow, white cloths from Samoa and Fiji are frequently decorated with elegant and fine hand-drawn motifs in black. Although each pattern is unique, a small group of usually abstract shapes is frequently repeated and reinterpreted by the artist. The cloth on the left was collected in Apia, Western Samoa before World War I by Wesleyan missionary, Reverend F. Copeland. 299 x 32 cm. The middle cloth is unlocalised but the words painted on it, *"Manaima, Tua iafa, irevaeru, ana, Sisavaia, Fa'asatoaina, Siutu, Eseta"* indicate a Samoan origin. 460 x 50 cm.
The cloth on the right was recorded as collected in Fiji, some time before 1886. 635 x 75 cm.

Siapo mamanu, Samoa. Circular sheets with freehand concentric designs are an adaptation for the tourist market, intended as table covers or even floor mats. This example bears the printed label *"Leone Tutuila",* identifying the village in American Samoa where it was made.
155 cm diameter.

Right: *Siapo tasina,* Samoa. First rubbed on a very simple *upeti*, the dominant design on this tapa has been produced by freehand overpainting. 279 × 155 cm.

Below: *Siapo tasina,* Samoa. Repeated freehand overpainting on a large rectangular leaf design tablet has produced a strangely disturbing symmetry. 169 × 156 cm.

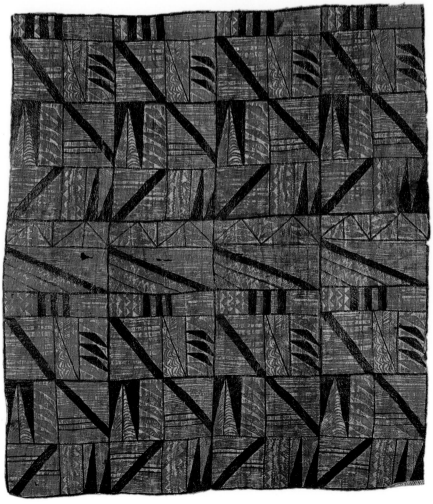

Right: *Siapo mamanu*, Samoa. A good example of Leone village style design, featuring the popular early twentieth-century Leone motif derived from the shape of breadfruit leaves. This cloth was obtained in Apia, Western Samoa, but was obviously made in Leone, American Samoa. 278 × 224 cm.

Below: *Siapo tasina*, Samoa. This tapa has been decorated by serial rubbing on a rectangular leaf design tablet, then the design has been emphasized by repeated and restrained minimal overpainting. The characteristic Samoan motif of an overpainted dark-brown circle with central white spot completes the pattern. 196 × 132 cm.

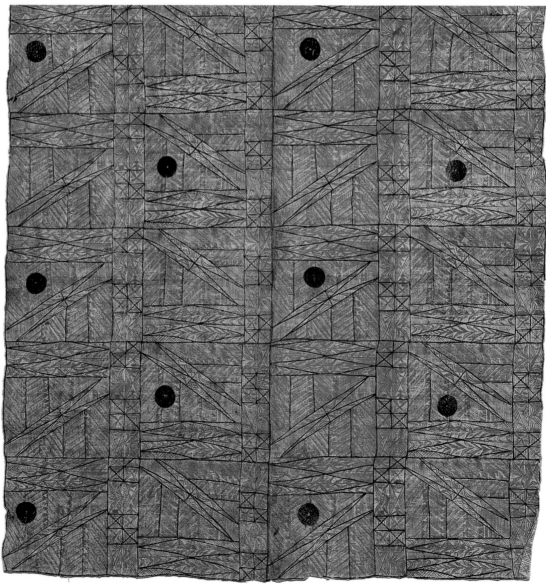

Siapo vala, Samoa. A bold design produced by strong overpainting on a cloth rubbed on a large rectangular carved wooden design tablet. 149 × 145 cm.

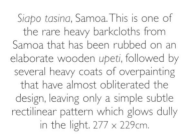

Siapo tasina, Samoa. This is one of the rare heavy barkcloths from Samoa that has been rubbed on an elaborate wooden *upeti*, followed by several heavy coats of overpainting that have almost obliterated the design, leaving only a simple subtle rectilinear pattern which glows dully in the light. 277 × 229cm.

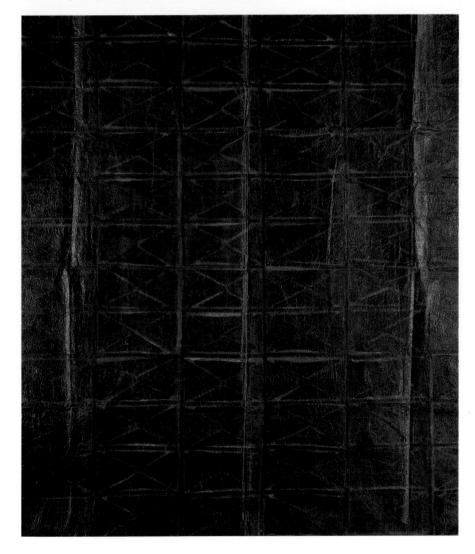

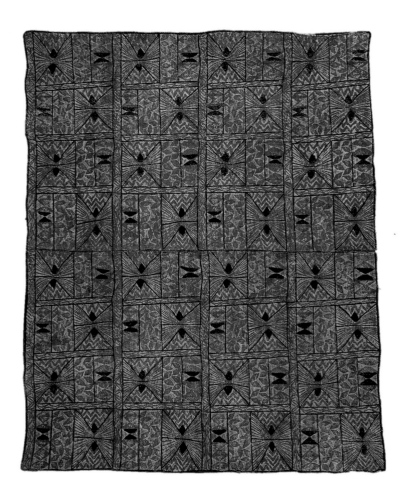

Left: *Siapo tasina,* Samoa. James Edge-Partington obtained this tapa cloth from the collection of Robert Louis Stevenson. 183 × 150 cm.

Opposite: *Siapo tasina,* Samoa. Very large sheets of tapa were often left completed at this stage, after being rubbed on a leaf *upeti,* without any overpainting being applied. 393 × 329 cm.

Below: *Siapo mamanu,* Samoa (detail). 141 × 120 cm.

Above: *Siapo tasina*, Samoa. 211 x 148 cm.

Left: *Siapo tasina*, Samoa. Recorded as being
collected in Niue, this tapa – with its leaf design
tablet imprint and freehand overpainting – is
clearly of Samoan origin. 195 x 157 cm.

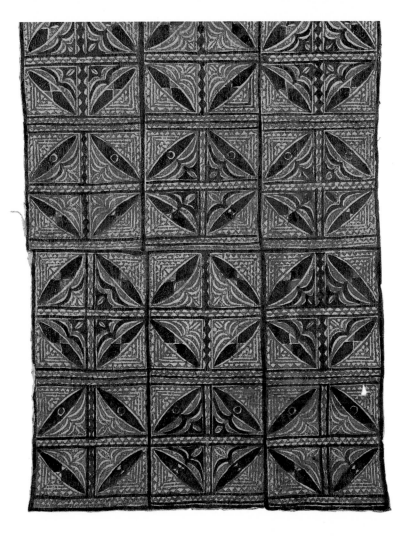

Siapo vala, Samoa. Collected in Samoa in 1958, this is the type of *siapo* that was used at that time for ceremonial presentations to titled chiefs. Cloths like this are also worn by orators. Decorated on a carved wooden design tablet, the pattern has been emphasized by freehand overpainting. A view of the back of this sheet (below) shows the original wooden *upeti* pattern without any overpainting. 164 x 120 cm.

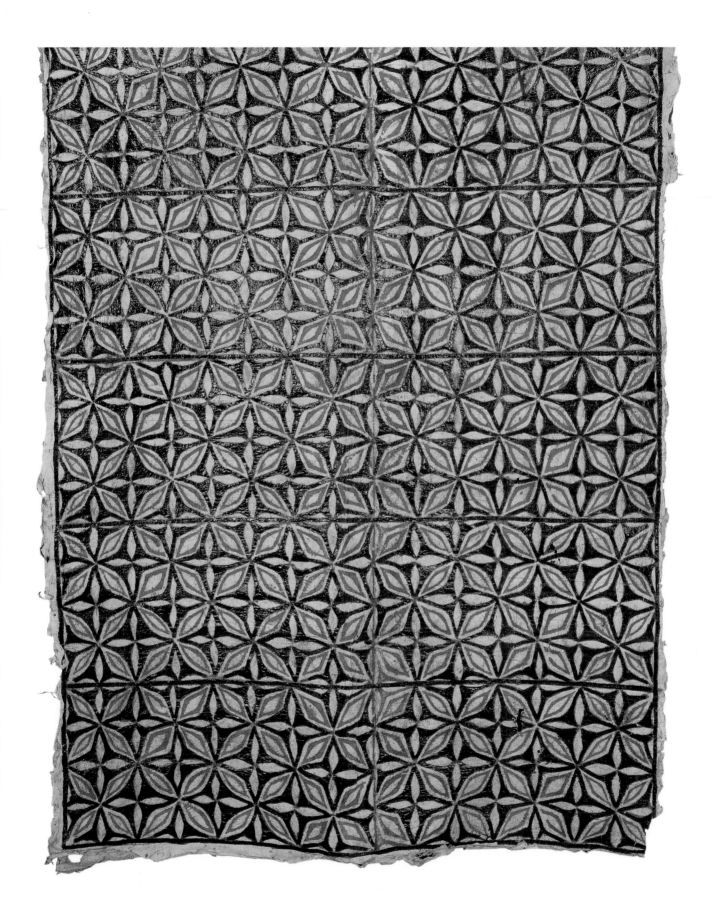

Siapo vala, Samoa. A *siapo* with a striking pattern
produced by careful intensive overpainting on a
simple design imprinted from a wooden carved
upeti. 169 × 130 cm.

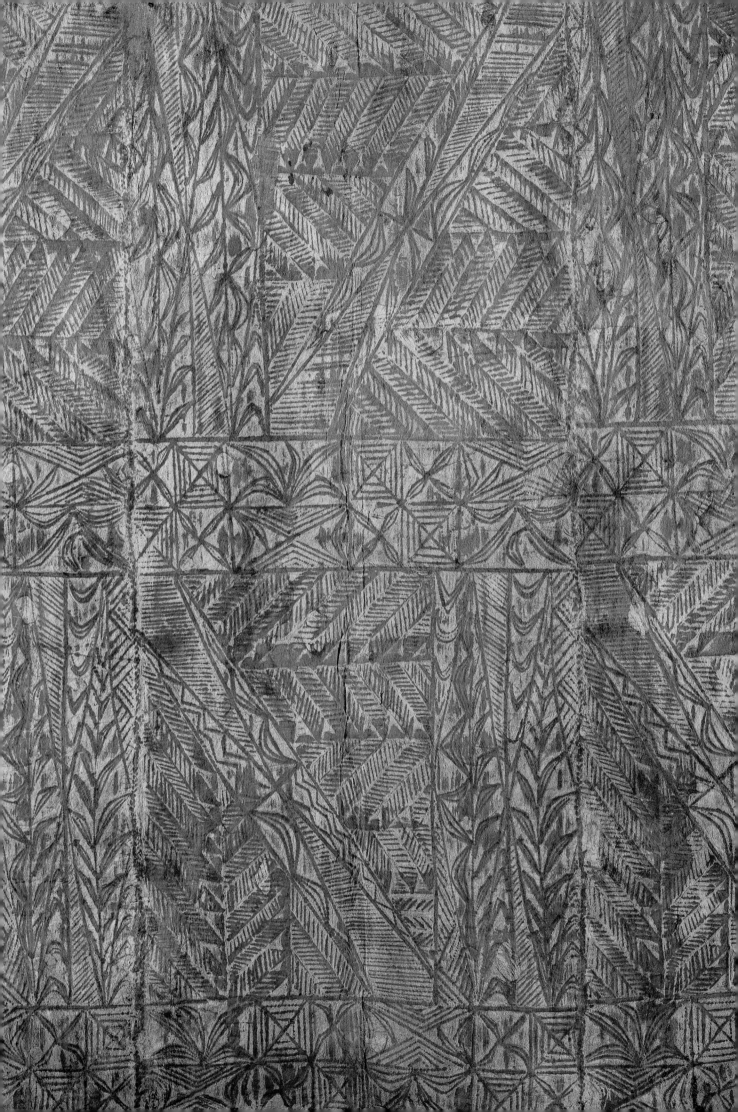

CHAPTER 4

TONGA

Beating tapa, 1890s, Tongatapu, Tonga. Tongan women often worked on the tapa in groups to relieve the tedium of the beating process.

Opposite: *Ngatu,* Tonga. Designs are applied to Tongan *ngatu* by laying the cloth over a *kupesi* pattern block and rubbing the cloth with a wad of pigmented tapa. Older *kupesi* are made from short lengths of coconut frond leaflet midrib sewn on to a foundation of palm spathe or pandanus leaves. Early patterns are complex, usually abstract and often left without any overpainting, as with this example. 340 x 198 cm.

In the Kingdom of Tonga most of the people live in the eastern chain of raised coral islands, including the Vava'u group with Niuafo'ou and Niuatoputapu to the north, the Ha'apai group, and larger Tongatapu in the south – the latter being the cultural and population centre for the entire group. The western chain is of volcanic origin with small and largely unpopulated islands.

The climate and soils of Tongatapu are particularly suitable for the cultivation of paper mulberry and it is here that most Tongan tapa or *ngatu* is produced. In the Ha'apai group and Niuatoputapu, where paper mulberry cannot be grown, the people have specialised in the production of fine plaited mats and these are traded to Tongatapu in exchange for tapa.

An early nineteenth-century record notes the use of breadfruit to produce a particular type of cloth used in funerals, but at the present time paper mulberry is used exclusively. After beating the bast on a long wooden anvil called a *tutua*, the next stage is that of joining and patterning which assembles the small pieces of beaten cloth, *feta'aki*, into the full-sized *ngatu*. The work is done by a group of women working on a convex bench to which the patterned rubbing blocks, or *kupesi*, made of leaf strips are bound. The women seat themselves in pairs facing each other across the bench. First they spread two strips of *feta'aki* lengthwise between each pair of women and rub the surface of the cloth with brown pigment made from the bark of the *koka* tree (*Bischofia javanica*). Half-cooked arrowroot tubers are then rubbed across as a bonding agent. Next, a second pair of *feta'aki* are added, but this time at right angles to the first pair. The surface is rubbed again and then a new layer of dye rubbed on to bring out the pattern from the *kupesi* below.

Above: Demonstration of tapa decorating, 1930s, Nukualofa, Tonga. As one of the most distinctive Pacific crafts, tapa-making has often been demonstrated at public occasions. Here, Tongan women pose with their equipment for rubbing the cloth on *kupesi*.

Left: Beating tapa, 1987, Houma village, Tongatapu, Tonga. Working in the shade, this woman has her wooden anvil raised off the ground for comfort and resonance. Taken almost one hundred years after the photo on the previous page, this scene illustrates the persistence of tapa manufacturing techniques.

When all of the pairs of women have completed this process the finished section is pulled across by the women on the other side and the process is repeated. This joining, pasting and rubbing continues until the *ngatu* has reached its required length. A white undyed border, which is left at each side, is known in Tongan as *tapa*. As each section is passed over the bench it is the job of the woman at each end to record the total number of completed units. The unit for counting is *langanga*, a measuring unit used for barkcloth which is based on half the width of the rubbing bench, usually between 45 and 60 cm (1 to 2 feet). The completed cloth will be at least fifty *langanga* long – and sometimes much longer.

The final stage of manufacture takes place after the cloth has been dried in the sun, then put under the sleeping mat and slept on for several nights to flatten it. When she is ready, the owner spreads the whole cloth out and highlights the patterns by overpainting with brown or black dye. For this she uses the dried key of a pandanus fruit, sharpened to a point to form a paint brush. Certain kinds of *ngatu*, however, are considered finished when the ribbed pattern has been applied and no overpainting is required.

A very wide range of motifs is used in Tonga, both abstract and naturalistic, sometimes with printed text included in the borders of designs. Tonga is one of the

Ngatu, Tonga. This tapa was printed from
a range of *kupesi* rubbing tablets, with
some of them darkened with heavier
rubbing. No overpainting has been added.
370 × 183 cm.

Ngatu, Auckland / Tonga. A barkcloth made by the Tongan community in Auckland during a Polynesian display, May 1966, to demonstrate the traditional method of manufacture. The materials were brought from Vava'u, and later the cloth was sent to Tonga for the black overpainting to be applied. 392 × 238 cm.

few, or even, perhaps, the only culture in the Pacific where historical events are commemorated in tapa motifs. Thus, the popular representation of a shooting star dates from the appearance of Halley's Comet over Tonga in 1910, while the installation of electric lighting in the streets of Nukualofa has been shown on some cloths by a line of power poles among the Norfolk pines of the *Hala Paini*. Royal Coats of Arms, marking the date of specific coronations, may also be included in this category. Even the wartime RAF fighter planes, paid for by Tongan contributions to Britain, have been remembered in tapa decoration. Perhaps the antique wind-up gramophone and bicycle seen on some tapa also mark a more personal historical experience for their designers.

The people of Tonga have worn Western-style clothing for many years, although the wrap-around cloth for men has persisted, and for important and ceremonial occasions a variety of waist mats are worn. Tapa appears as costume for dance groups and the bride and groom may wear it with their fine mats for a traditional Tongan-

A young couple of high rank, 1880, Tonga. With their traditional hairstyles and ornaments of a comb and boar's tusk, this young couple pose in barkcloth garments which have been patterned on leaf *kupesi*. Around her waist the woman has added a rare piece of Tongan dark tapa, or *ngatu'uli*, of the type exchanged between bride and groom at their wedding.

style wedding. Although tapa is now seldom worn as clothing, it is still an extremely important element of the culture and huge amounts continue to be manufactured. Tongans are the most prolific tapa producers in the Pacific – and indeed in the world. Tapa has retained its importance for gifts and exchanges at traditional ceremonies. The pathway of important guests may be laid with *ngatu* so that they walk on it. Large amounts are required for the celebration of births and weddings, and also for funerals – especially when connected to the royal family, nobles or other families of importance. On these occasions a single *ngatu* cloth may reach up to 100 metres in length and cloths a mile long have been recorded. The presentation of large pieces is a spectacular sight as they move forward supported by a long line of women at each side.

Display of traditional wealth, 1920s, Tonga. Probably assembled for a wedding exchange, this display of traditional wealth includes several headrests, woven items, fine Tongan baskets containing bottles of scented coconut oil, and two large bundles of tapa cloth loosely wrapped in plaited mats.

Following spread: Tongan tapa decorative motifs.

ELIZABETH
1953

Above: *Ngatu*, Tonga. The *kupesi* motifs here have been inspired by Queen Salote's royal regalia. 431 × 195 cm.

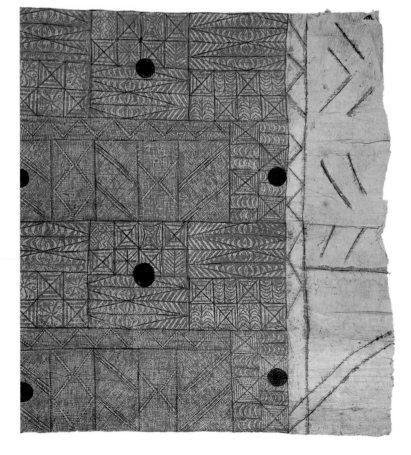

Left: *Ngatu*, Tonga. A *ngatu* patterned from *kupesi* rubbing tablets and then finely painted with black outlines and round spots. The elongated diamond-shaped motif is known in Tongan as *tokelau feletoa*. 329 × 71 cm.

Above: *Ngatu,* Tonga. A *ngatu* with naturalistic plant motifs. The rubbing tablet has been bound with cords which provide the lined brown background. Then the *kupesi* rubbing tablets have been placed on top of these cords so that both the lines and motifs are printed in a single process. The white section has been carefully rubbed according to the *tapa'ingatu* process, so that only the motifs and brown grid have taken the colour, leaving the surrounding cloth white. 237 × 212 cm.

Right: *Ngatu,* Tonga. A comparatively simple rubbed rectilinear pattern with black overpainting. Collected in the 1970s by Gordon Skipper of Volunteer Service Abroad. 378 × 164 cm.

Left: *Ngatu,* Tonga. In the making of this *ngatu,* the convex working tablet has been wrapped with cords with a set of *kupesi* rubbing tablets placed on top. The rubbing recorded the cords as parallel lines with the *kupesi* motifs spaced across them. The motifs were then highlighted by painting some parts brown and outlining in black. This piece was collected in Tonga about 1971. 458 × 230 cm.

Below: *Ngatu,* Tonga. The lightly rubbed pattern on this *ngatu* is outlined in black, and black details have been painted in. Among the motifs is a row of buildings and a row of trees. The latter is identified in the script as "*Hala Paini*", the avenue of Norfolk pines that lines the way to the royal palace in Nukualofa. 222 × 210 cm.

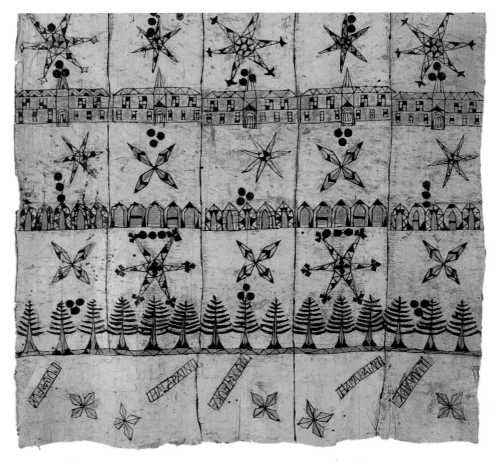

Ngatu, Tonga. This *ngatu* features naturalistic impressions
of fish rubbed from two *kupesi* tablets. Variations on the
basic designs were then developed by overpainting.
The cloth was collected by Reverend Robert Gordon-Kingan,
who lived in Tonga from 1927 to 1932. 430 x 134 cm.

Right: *Ngatu*, Tonga. This *ngatu* has been decorated with an unusual pattern lightly rubbed from a *kupesi* and then precisely overpainted in brown and outlined in black. 372 x 240 cm.

Below right: *Ngatu*, Tonga. This tapa was made at a community centre where girls were taught the art of *ngatu* production. The *kupesi* from which the pattern was rubbed appears to be constructed from lengths of stick, thicker than usual, or perhaps strips of bamboo. This motif is known in Tonga as *kalou*. Details have been painted in black. The tapa was collected in about 1966. 179 x 117 cm.

Opposite: *Ngatu*, Tonga. The lines applied from a *kupesi* rubbing tablet have been used as the foundation for this strongly overpainted pattern outlined in black. Alternating with the bands of chevron patterns are bands of the pattern called *manulua*, based on the so-called "vane swastika", which is a very widespread motif in the Pacific. 277 x 236 cm.

Dance tunic, Tonga. A child's dance tunic painted
with a scene of two aeroplanes attacking the
rising sun, probably a symbolic allusion to the RAF
fighter planes purchased with funds contributed
by the people of Tonga. 45 × 42 cm.

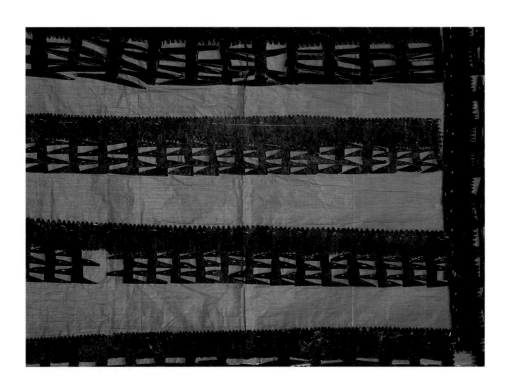

Above: Dance skirt, Tonga. Skirts like this are worn
by young Tongan women when dancing at Tongan
festivals. Cut-outs of black tapa have been sewn
on to blue cotton cloth. 84 × 60 cm.

Opposite: *Ngatu*, Tonga. A large tapa with sparsely
spaced motifs applied from a *kupesi* tablet, and
then painted brown with black details. This is a
tapa'ingatu produced by rubbing only over the
actual *kupesi*, leaving the rest of the cloth
uncoloured. 1001 × 432 cm.

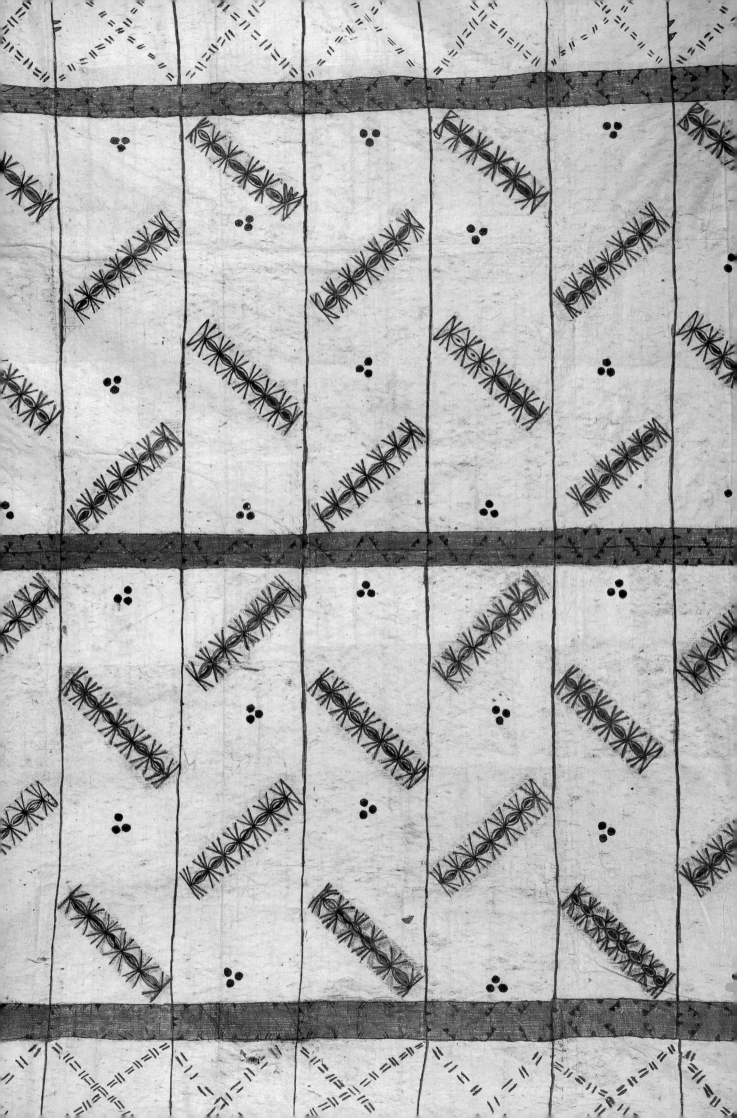

Kupesi, rubbing tablet, Tonga. Constructed on a base of pandanus leaves, the design on the front is outlined by coconut leaf midribs stitched in place with coir fibre. 45 x 21 cm.

Kupesi, rubbing tablet, Tonga. Made on a base of coconut leaf sheaths, the design is outlined by coconut leaf midribs stitched in place with coir. 45 x 31 cm.

Kupesi, rubbing tablet, Tonga. Made on a base of pandanus leaves, the design is outlined by coconut leaf midribs stitched in place with coir. Subsidiary design lines are created by lines of string stitching. 49 x 12 cm.

Kupesi, rubbing tablet, Tonga. Made on a base of coconut leaf sheath, the design on this tablet is outlined by coconut leaf midribs stitched in place with coir. 72 x 23 cm.

Right: *Kupesi*, rubbing tablet, Tonga. Representing a coat of arms, this elaborate *kupesi* is made on a base of coconut leaf sheath, with the design outlined with coconut leaf midribs stitched in place with coir. Subsidiary design lines are created by lines of string stitching. 51 x 39 cm.

Below right: *Ike*, tapa beaters, Tonga. Made from hard *toa* wood, with their typical tapered shape, one of these beaters has a smooth facet, the other has very wide grooves on all surfaces. 29.5 cm long.

Following pages: *Ngatu,* Tonga. A *kupesi*-patterned cloth richly decorated with the *Sila o Tonga* (the Tongan coat of arms), *Hala Paini* (the Norfolk pines growing along the road leading to the palace), the British royal lion, the aristocratic eagle, and the dove of peace. Variations on this design have been among the most popular patterns produced in the second half of the nineteenth century. Tongan tapa with these motifs then became very popular during World War II, expressing Tongan solidarity with Britain. 456 x 225 cm.

CHAPTER 5

UVEA (WALLIS ISLAND)

About 9,000 people live on Uvea; the residents are Polynesians who speak a language closely related to Tongan. Although Uvea is of volcanic origin, it is in fact rather low and flat and does not attract a high rainfall. On the east coast, where rainfall is highest, there is tropical vegetation and the paper mulberry is cultivated for tapa-making.

Their general name for tapa is *ngatu*. The term *holo* is applied to large sheets used as bed covers and screens. These large, double-layer cloths are pasted together and boldly painted freehand, or patterned from a rubbing tablet, and then overpainted. The rubbing tablets are made of either wads of leaf with midribs sewn into place to form the patterns, or carved wooden tablets – the latter being the more recent form.

The barkcloth *lafi* is a wrap-around skirt decorated by rubbing over a pattern block and then overpainting. Another type of wrap-around skirt is known as *tohihina*. Its decoration is all applied freehand; fine black motifs are drawn with a pen on a white background.

During the second half of the twentieth century a new figurative style appeared. Naturalistic renderings of daily activities are the main theme, showing people gathering and preparing food, climbing trees, drinking *kava* and dancing, or alternatively, fishing from a canoe when particular attention and realistic detail is given to the underwater life.

Opposite: *Ngatu,* Uvea. On the basis of comparison with documented examples, this old cloth, with fine freehand painted black patterns is considered to be from Uvea. 197 x 139 cm.

CHAPTER 6
FUTUNA

The Polynesian people of Futuna now living on the islands number about 5,000, and speak a language closely related to Samoan. Futuna and its sister island Alofi are both high volcanic islands, with fertile soil and high rainfall permitting abundant growth of tropical plants including *lafi,* the local name for the paper mulberry which is used for making tapa.

Some of the finest detail on any tapa is found on the Futuna waist garments known as *salatasi* which are made by an individual working alone. Two layers of tapa are felted together into a single thin but firm layer, which is divided into pattern areas, most of which are ruled up with a remarkable grid of very fine black lines using a narrow pen cut from a coconut frond midrib. Selected areas of the grid are painted with red-brown or black pigments creating the thicker lines and shapes which form the pattern. Small freehand motifs may be placed on or between the ruled grid areas. The patterned area is often surrounded by a fringe made by cutting into the border with sometimes simple – but frequently ornate – decoration.

Siapo, the general name used locally for tapa, is also used to describe the large sheets of softer cloth made by a group of women working together. In this case, the two layers of cloth are pasted together over the underside of the hull of an old canoe and patterned with rubbed decorations from design tablets similar to those used in Tonga. They are then boldly overpainted. Some appear to be painted entirely freehand and surprisingly, when contrasted with the fineness and formality of the *salatasi* skirt patterns, include some of the most uninhibited and freely painted patterns of the Pacific.

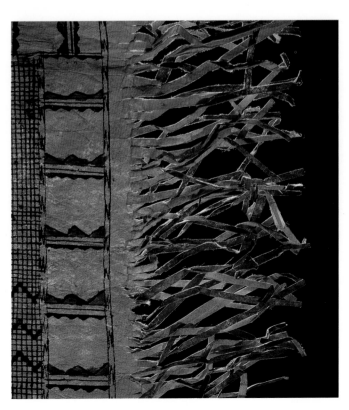

Opposite: *Salatasi*, tapa waist mat, Futuna. This pattern is based on precisely drawn fine black lines with small areas painted brown. The "vane swastika", or windmill motif, forming the central panel is common on tapa from Tonga, Samoa and Fiji and appears as far afield as Sulawesi in Indonesia. Three sides are decorated with cut fringes. 145 × 117 cm.

The detail at right shows a section of side fringe which is often a feature of *salatasi*. The reverse of the cloth has been stained brown, adding colour interest to the fringe.

Right: *Lafi*, tapa bandolier, Nuku village, Futuna. This long strip of white tapa is used in dance performances. It is worn over one shoulder and secured at the waist beneath the other. This is a typical example, with a fringe at each end made by cutting slits in the cloth. The fringes and the adjacent areas are decorated with finely drawn patterns in black, while the central section carries more sparse decoration. This was purchased at the 1992 Festival of Pacific Arts, Rarotonga, Cook Islands. 390 × 41 cm.

Above: Dancers from Futuna at the 1996 Festival of Pacific Arts, Apia, Western Samoa. The dress of these dancers consists entirely of newly made tapa, from the white turban to the *lafi* bandolier and the *tepi* skirt.

The *tepi*, a wrap-around skirt worn by men as a dancing costume, is also partly decorated by rubbing the cloth over a leaf design tablet attached to the curve of a canoe hull. It is then overpainted, the main outlines being highlighted in black, but with rather more care than is used for the larger sheets. The wide lower border of the skirt is hand-painted with fine patterns again applied with a bamboo pen. The *lafi*, a long narrow strip worn by the men across the shoulder and chest, are decorated at each end with fine freehand patterns in black. Most of the length of the strip is white with widely spaced motifs in black. At each end there are cut fringes of wide strips which are also usually painted with black patterns.

The same costume may be worn by women but at other times the women's dance costume is a hand-painted tapa tunic worn over a matching skirt of the same material. Both are decorated with cut tapa fringes, or attached fringes of brightly coloured fibre.

Above: *Tepi*, tapa skirt, Ono village, Futuna. Fine hand-painted patterns persist on the lower borders of tapa skirts and are combined with much bolder freehand painting, which decorates the rest of the cloth. This example was worn by a male dancer, Masei Malino, at the 1992 Festival of Pacific Arts, Rarotonga, Cook Islands. 194 × 118 cm.

Right: A hand-painted motif from the lower border of the *tepi* dance skirt.

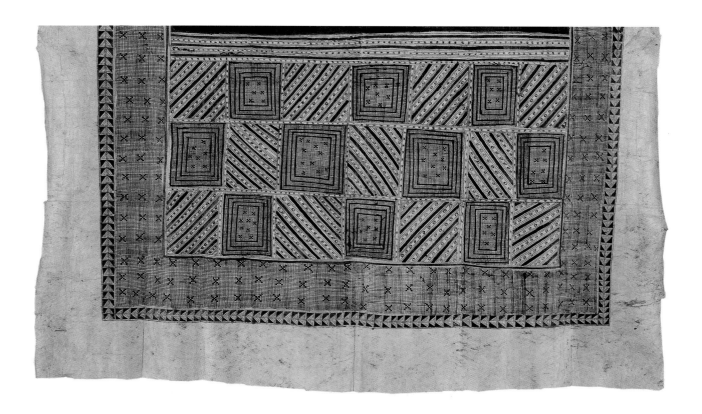

Above: *Salatasi*, tapa waist mat, Futuna. This tapa
depicts another arrangement with the three-sided
border around a finely decorated central
checkerboard panel with concentric squares and
diagonal lines. 78 × 138 cm.

Below: A detail shows a small rectangle of
diagonal drawn lines with brown and black
painted areas.

Opposite: *Siapo*, Mala'e village, Futuna. This large
cloth with its bold painting was purchased from
a member of the Futuna contingent at the
1992 Festival of Pacific Arts, Rarotonga,
Cook Islands. 437 × 239 cm.

67

CHAPTER 7

NIUE

Ceremonial challenge, 1900s, Niue. This rare photograph of Niueans wearing tapa shows a ceremonial challenge between men armed with Niuean clubs and spears. The man on the left wears a *lavalava* of freehand painted *hiapo* with a Samoan pattern.

Ike, tapa beaters, Niue. Among all the tapa beaters of the Pacific islands, those of Niue are among the most elaborately carved and elegantly shaped. They display the raised zigzag cuff and incised patterns seen also on Niuean spears and clubs.
Left: 33 cm long. Right: 34 cm long.

Opposite: *Hiapo*, Niue. A freehand painted *hiapo* with plant forms and abstract patterns. Small motifs are used to fill spaces. Inscriptions on the border read, "*Laifone mai puka. Te mu ki tai. Ikipa Lulai 13 1886.*" 246 × 200 cm.

Niue is an upraised atoll surrounded by rugged cliffs which make landing difficult. When Captain Cook reached the island in 1774, a combination of the cliffs and a ferocious reception from the people made landing impossible. Reports of Cook's experiences discouraged other visitors, and it was not until the visit of Reverend John Williams of the London Missionary Society in 1830 that communication began and missionaries from Samoa were landed.

There is virtually no information available on ancient Niuean tapa, except for Williams's mention of an old man wearing "a narrow strip of cloth", and no examples of early pieces have survived in collections. In an effort to make the people cover their bodies, Samoan missionaries are said to have taught them Samoan methods of making tapa, and introduced the *tiputa*, a poncho which had already been introduced to Samoa from Tahiti. The decoration on these is painted freehand, with many elements reminiscent of Samoan patterns, but apparently none were decorated by the Samoan rubbing method. Some tapa cloth in early photographs and examples said to have been collected in Niue, however, are indistinguishable from Samoan tapa of the same period. They may have been imported by the missionaries, made by missionary wives or perhaps made by Niuean women working with them.

In the 1880s a striking new indigenous style suddenly appeared, developing and refining the patterns which had already appeared on *tiputa*. Contained within a rectangular or circular format, the patterns are very distinctive; abstract shapes and plant forms delicately drawn with fine black lines and usually set on a grid. The motifs are usually small, carefully arranged to fill planned spaces, and meticulously painted. Occasionally, naive naturalistic paintings of men or women in western dress appear. Small stars, leaves and naturalistic representations of fish may be used to fill

Left: *Hiapo,* Niue. A square *hiapo* divided into concentric circles which are almost entirely filled with fine hand-painted black patterns depicting plant motifs. Small stars, leaf shapes and a small fish are used as space fillers. A printed word appears in one corner. 192 x 174 cm.

Opposite: *Hiapo,* Niue. This is a fine example of the striking new *hiapo* style that suddenly appeared in Niue during the 1880s. The patterns are very distinctive, mainly abstract shapes and plant forms painted with fine black lines and arranged on a grid. The script on the border is not easy to read as some letters cannot be identified, while others are upside-down or back to front. The words appear to be *"T. Lipa mata 1855 Tavatu T Hapuku I opi i ana 1885 i niue mai puka. Mosoiamo i ai Foni Ktiona. Laifone."* This text probably identifies the makers, the village and date of manufacture. 261 x 236 cm.

small gaps, and often personal names and place-names are painted on the border. The unity of style, repeated use of motifs and frequent reappearance of some of the names suggest they were all made in a single close-knit community. Within that community there was undoubtedly a strong creative personality and leader who planned designs and supervised their production. The texture of the cloth is also quite different from Samoan tapa, being thicker, stiffer, and felted together into a single sheet rather than pasted in the west Polynesian manner. This use of a felting technique may suggest some influence from the Cook Islands. Apart from being so stiff, their large size and shape make them inappropriate for clothing, and the purpose for which they were made remains a mystery. There is a possibility that they were made at a church

Following pages: Niuean tapa decorative motifs.

training centre or some similar organisation and intended to be sold through church connections to raise funds or presented to dignitaries. Whatever the case, by 1901 when Percy Smith, the first New Zealand Government Resident arrived, production had ended and no tapa at all was being made.

Niuean tapa beaters are also very distinctive. They are somewhat similar to those of Samoa with a square section and flared end. However, the grooving is much finer than that on Samoan and Tongan beaters and there is a zigzag cuff between the handle and the beating end, which is apparently unique to Niue. Sometimes there are patterns marked in lines of fine dot incisions which, along with the zigzag cuff, are also found on spears and clubs from the island.

CHAPTER 8

COOK ISLANDS

Opposite: *Tiputa*, Aitutaki, Cook Islands. Long cut fringes are typical of *tiputa* worn as dance costume at the turn of the century. This one is decorated with freehand painting on deeply ridged cloth. Total length 114 x 38 cm at shoulder.

On the small atolls of the northern Cook Islands, where the barkcloth tree will not grow because of low rainfall and poor sandy soil, the people developed very fine plaitwork which served their needs for clothing. But in the high volcanic islands to the south, which attract rain and where the soil is rich, tapa-making for clothing and other purposes was widespread and a number of different styles became established. Paper mulberry was the usual source of tapa, but breadfruit and banyan also provided some tapa material. Decoration of Cook Islands tapa was by freehand painting, dyeing by immersion in vegetable dyes or swamp mud, or in a few cases by stamping with a frame – as on Aitutaki. The western Polynesian technique of rubbing over a design tablet was never used in the Cook Islands.

One type of cloth made in large rectangular sheets, although left uncoloured and undecorated, is quite distinctive, with delicate ribbing from the imprint of finely grooved beaters. The direction of the fibre in this cloth is also unusual. Sometimes it all runs in one direction, as would be expected when the bark is torn from the plant. However, in other cloths it runs in two directions, suggesting that during the beating a subsequent layer was laid and felted at right angles to the foundation layer. In yet others, the fibres are arranged haphazardly. In all of these, even when the cloth is large, there is no sign of any joins and the fibres are completely felted together into a single layer. Tapa cloth of this type is especially characteristic of Mangaia island, Cook Islands, where it is recorded that a special thick white cloth called *tikoru* was made by men rather than women. This thick white cloth was employed as a covering for the images of the gods and was also worn by high chiefs and priests.

In Rarotonga, carved god staffs of wood, some up to 4 metres (13 feet) long and others quite small, were wrapped in tapa, with the ends of the carving projecting from each opening. The tapa wrapped around these staffs is soft with a smooth surface. It is decorated with a black or black and brown pattern, usually repetitive and sometimes with vigorous cross-hatching in which the pattern is hardly discernable until the cloth is held to the light. On conversion to Christianity these figures were offered up to the missionaries for destruction (although some were reputedly hidden away in caves). Examples were sent to England as visible proof of the success of the mission. The unintended but fortunate result was the survival of fine examples of god images intended for suppression which are now displayed in museums and admired with an enthusiasm the mission could not have predicted. Fortunately, some of these have even retained their tapa cloth wrappings. Other minor gods were represented by small objects made of tapa cloth, feathers and human hair or coconut fibre.

Ponchos (known by their Tahitian name, *tiputa*) were probably introduced by missionaries of the London Missionary Society from Tahiti in order to encourage their converts to cover their bodies and were made in the southern Cook Islands. However, there are also some indications that the poncho may have been worn in both the southern Cook Islands and Tahiti in pre-European times, probably as a mourning dress by higher ranking people. Some ponchos made in the Cook Islands

Left: Surrender of traditional gods, 1820s, Rarotonga, Cook Islands. After their conversion to Christianity, the people of Rarotonga delivered their god staff images, still wrapped in tapa, to the European missionaries.

Below: Opening scene of an *eva* pageant, 1903, Mangaia or Rarotonga, Cook Islands. Male dancers dressed in tapa costumes and masks prepare to dance with their long *korare* spears.

were decorated with painted patterns, while others were dyed entirely red, black or yellow. On Mangaia, especially, small angular perforations cut through the cloth and arranged in decorative rows imparted a lacy look to the poncho. Sometimes, perforated cloths dyed one colour were pasted over another plain cloth of contrasting colour so that the second colour showed through the openwork. Usually the borders were decorated with long fringes, often cut into complex shapes.

Even after the complete acceptance of woven cloth, *tiputa* made from tapa continued to be produced for use as costumes in local celebrations and festivals until the early twentieth century. The marking of popular occasions or visits of important celebrities has continued to initiate enthusiastic experimentations in dress and reinterpretations of the past. A number of these garments have survived in museum collections. They include ponchos with long fringes and openwork, shirts and trousers made from barkcloth with painted patterns and – a new departure for Polynesia – barkcloth masks.

Very little is known about the exact origin of these Mangaian tapa masks called *pare eva* or *pare tareka* – which is frustrating, especially in view of the rarity of masks in Polynesia. The word *eva* relates to mourning ceremonies, while *tareka* suggests festive dancing. Most of the information has been gleaned from a few rare period

Above: God staff with tapa wrapping, Rarotonga, Cook Islands. One of the smaller Rarotongan god staffs collected by early missionaries, this example has retained its original tapa wrapping. Protected within this wrapping were the symbols of the spirit of the god in the form of red feathers and a string of pearl shell discs. The god represented is probably Tangaroa, the creator god of the Cook Islanders. 74 cm long x 9 cm diameter.

Left: Tapa cloth wrapping from god staff, Rarotonga, Cook Islands. A subtle dark criss-cross pattern in black and red has been painted in bands along the central portion of the tapa wrapping of the god staff. The resulting diamond-shaped motifs are associated with the sacred world of the gods. 581 x 50 cm.

photographs that show them in use. Tapa masks seem to have developed on Mangaia in the 1880s and 1890s, perhaps stimulated by Cook Islander missionaries returning from Melanesia where they would have encountered many different forms of masks. Most of the Mangaian masks were conical or partly square, with open slits for eyes and mouth, but others were more elaborate constructions of tapa, wood and feathers. Another form, with a moulded, more naturalistic face and large ears, shows some similarity to New Britain and New Ireland masks.

Masks were apparently worn in pageants or tableau called *eva* commemorating the actions of gods and culture heroes. They were also perhaps of a historical nature, illustrating the spread of Christianity through the Pacific. Accompanied by slit gong

Above: Actors in *eva* costume, 1903, Mangaia or Rarotonga, Cook Islands. Men and women pose with their barkcloth *eva* costumes, some holding the slit gongs that provide musical accompaniment to the performance.

Left: *Ike*, tapa beaters, Cook Islands. Tapa beaters in the Cook Islands were made from *toa* wood according to the usual eastern Polynesian long narrow form, with four parallel sides and a wide range of grooving – from very fine to very wide. Lengths from top, 41.5 cm, 42.6 cm, 42.8 cm.

music, men and women wearing masks and tapa costumes danced with long spears until a final scene where they all appear unmasked. These pageants were also performed on Rarotonga, but probably by Mangaians resident there.

There are elements in this masking complex which relate back to the old indigenous traditions and religion of Mangaia. The name of the pageants in which they were worn, called *eva*, suggests that they were based on the solemn old traditional *eva* ceremonies which were part of the mourning ritual for a great chief. A photograph dating from 1906 features two impressive masked figures, with a caption reading "Mangaians in gala dress with their gods Avatea and Tangiia". Avatea – or Vatea – the largest figure, whose name means "the bright light of noon or daylight", was the primal being who split open the rock and allowed the departmental gods to emerge. Tangiia was the mythical fourth son of this Vatea, not to be confused with the legendary Tangiia, who discovered many islands.

Some tapa masks and dance costumes of this Mangaian type were collected by Auckland Museum staff in Arorangi village on Rarotonga in 1899. Mangaian participants at the 1906 South Seas International Exhibition held in Christchurch, New Zealand wore conical tapa masks and ponchos, several of which ended up in New Zealand museum collections.

Tiputa, Rarotonga, Cook Islands. Although the *tiputa* tunic had been introduced to the Cook Islands, it was soon adopted as part of traditional dance costume for festive occasions. Here, the perforated cloth has been impregnated with a dye that has given it a shiny surface. Total length 207 × 149 cm.

More recently, beauty queen carnivals in New Zealand have attracted the attention of creative designers. The Miss Cook Islands category entails a costume that enshrines elements from the Cook Islands and its past. Tapa cloth is among the most persistent components and is used with a range of other Cook Island and Pan-Pacific features, such as bast fibre fringes and sea shells. Small sections or trimmings of tapa may be used as highlights on a ball gown or the fabric used in the dress might be printed with tapa patterns.

Left: *Pare eva*, barkcloth mask, Mangaia, Cook Islands. Mangaia is one of the rare places in Polynesia where masks were worn, by both men and women, with tapa costumes in dances at festivals. These Mangaian masks seem to be a late-nineteenth-century innovation on Mangaia, perhaps inspired by Cook Islander missionary experience of masked dancers in Melanesia. This one was collected by Te Rangi Hiroa (Sir Peter Buck), the prominent Maori anthropologist who did important field studies in the Cook Islands. 108 x 25 cm.

Below left: *Pare eva*, barkcloth mask, Rarotonga, Cook Islands. This mask was collected on Rarotonga in 1899, but it may have originated in Mangaia. This conical form is the most common type made for the *eva* dance pageants of the late nineteenth century. 87 x 31 cm.

Opposite: Tapa mask and costume, Rarotonga, Cook Islands. This unusual outfit of mask and costume was collected on Rarotonga, probably at Arorangi village, in 1899. For a short period in the late nineteenth and early twentieth centuries, Cook Island people on Mangaia and Rarotonga wore barkcloth masks and costumes in certain dances. With its fringed edges, the tunic shows some influence from earlier Cook Islands ponchos. Many of the patterns are derived from traditional Cook Island barkcloth decorative motifs. These costumes are evidence that the craft of making barkcloth was still active in Mangaia and perhaps Rarotonga, at least until the early years of this century. 200 x 89 cm wide at arms.

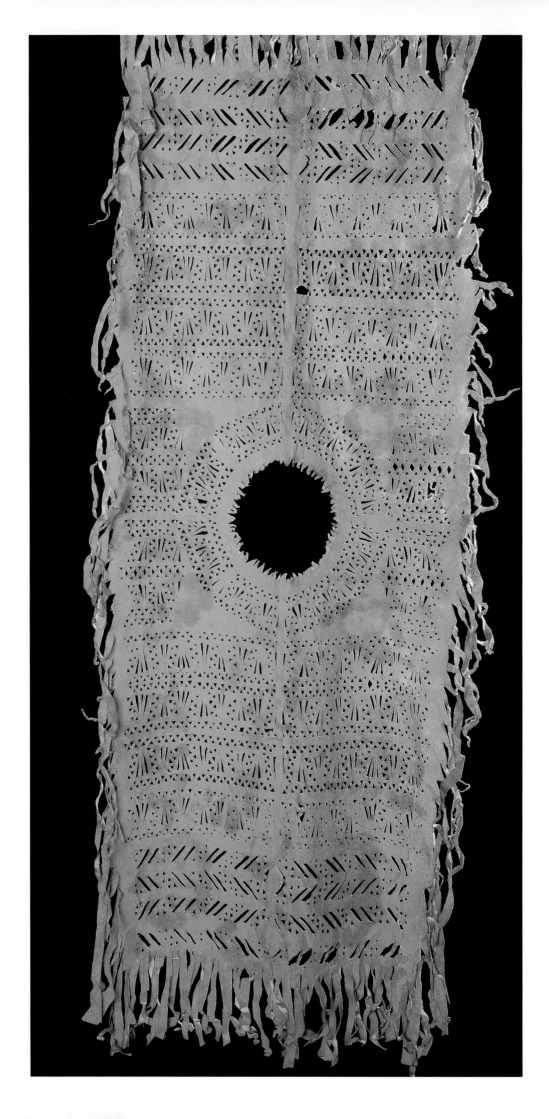

Opposite: *Tiputa*, Rarotonga, Cook Islands. Early missionaries probably introduced the poncho from Tahiti in an effort to cover the bodies of their converts. This *tiputa* has been dyed yellow, perhaps with turmeric, and decorated with intricate cut-out patterns. Although it was collected in Rarotonga in 1899 by the curator of Auckland Museum, these cut-out patterns suggest that it may have been made on Mangaia. 157 × 56 cm.

Below: *Tiputa* (detail), Rarotonga, Cook Islands. Some eastern Polynesian tapa shows fine cross-hatched lines in the texture of the cloth, as seen on this poncho. 157 × 56 cm.

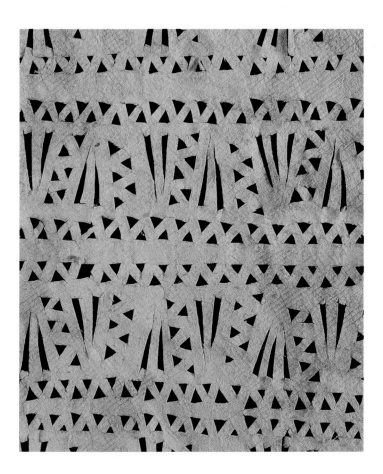

Right: Tapa textures, Cook Islands. In eastern Polynesia, where the fibres of tapa are carefully felted into a single layer, prominent texturing of undecorated cloth is a feature. This appears to be achieved by a combination of laying the fibres out in particular arrangements along with a textured surface decoration impressed from the pattern carved on the beater. The three examples illustrated are typical; (top) the fibres are at right angles to the parallel ridging of the beating; (middle) the fibre and the ridges are both arranged at approximate right angles; (bottom) the ridges and fibre are laid randomly.

CHAPTER 9

TAHITI

At least three different trees were used for making tapa in Tahiti: paper mulberry, breadfruit and two species of figs. Of these, paper mulberry was preferred. Large plantations of it were cultivated, to produce the favoured cloth of the upper classes. Commoners had to make use of the breadfruit tree. In a society as stratified as that of ancient Tahiti it also fell to the commoner to cultivate the plantations. This was done by the men, who also harvested the trees, and then handed the raw materials over to the women who did all the heavy and dirty work. The women would strip off their clothing and spend most of the day sitting in a flowing stream with a board on which they scraped away the rough outer bark. The strips were then laid out in an overlapping pattern two or three layers thick on a bed of banana leaves and left to drain overnight. By morning, the fibre had dried out to the extent that the pieces had stuck together and the entire strip was ready for beating. It was not until this process was completed and the cloth bleached in the sun that it was handed over to the upper-class women who would repair any blemishes and undertake the decoration.

Opposite: Tahitian tapa decorative motif.

For colours used in decoration, yellow was obtained from the tubers of the turmeric (*Curcuma* sp.) and roots of the *nono* (*Morinda*), which were usually employed as a dye to impregnate the whole cloth. A red colouring was produced by a complex and time-consuming process involving shaking droplets of juice from the stem of the mati fig (*Ficus tinctoria*) and steeping this liquid in a bowl of water containing leaves from the *etou* tree. In working with this colour the women's hands and fingernails became stained red, which was considered a mark of beauty and also indicated their rank. Brown and black dyes were produced in ways similar to those on other islands.

Tahitian tapa seen by the earliest European visitors was often dyed in solid colours by the immersion process, or left plain white. Other techniques of decoration became popular later.

Fibres stripped from a grass known as *mo'u* were used as paint brushes to apply fine lines and other motifs. Simple printing was done by using a length of bamboo, the circular end of which was dipped in the dye and then applied to the cloth.

Very soon after European contact there was an explosion in decorating techniques, perhaps stimulated by acquaintance with European printing methods. Leaves and fern fronds were dipped in dye and pressed against the cloth to leave their image, and cut-out patterns were pasted on to a surface of another colour. The fact that members of the *Arioi*, a society of travelling players, were masters of this kind of work suggests that this style of tapa perhaps served more as costume for entertainers than as ordinary everyday wear. Travelling between islands by canoe, the Arioi society consisted of young men and women entirely devoted to dance, song and pleasure in the name of Oro, their god. They gained the displeasure of missionaries because of their sexual freedom and their improvident way of life.

Most other tapa in Tahiti was worn by both men and women in the form of *tiputa*, or ponchos, either plain white or coloured red, black, brown or yellow. In

Left: Teremoemoe, widow of Pomare II of Tahiti, and Teffaaora, chief of Borabora, 1820s. Made of soft tapa cloth, both the *ahufara*, or shawl, of the woman and the *tiputa*, or poncho, of the man have been printed with fern leaf designs.

Left: *I'e*, tapa beater, Rurutu, Austral Islands, French Polynesia. Tapa beaters from the Austral Islands are very similar in shape to those made in Tahiti, the rest of French Polynesia, and the Cook Islands, which is to be expected in view of the cultural relationships between these island groups. 43 cm long.

Opposite: *Ahufara*, Tahiti. Worn as a shawl or scarf, this *ahufara* has a classical Tahitian tapa decoration pattern of printed fern and club moss motifs. These designs are produced by dipping the plant in dye and pressing it on the soft white felted tapa. 103 x 255 cm.

earlier times, plain yellow and red impregnated tapa was reserved for the ponchos of higher ranking people. The best *tiputa* were made of several paper-thin layers of tapa, beaten and pasted together with a top layer of very fine bleached tapa. Side-edges were decorated with fringes or feathers and sometimes a sash or belt was added around the waist. Under their *tiputa*, men wore a *maro* or loincloth of tapa while women wore a *pau* or *pareu* of tapa drawn around the waist and fastened at one side. An additional feminine item of clothing was the *ahufara*, a length of supple soft tapa worn as a shawl or scarf around the shoulders. Bales or bundles of fine white tapa up to 180 metres (590 feet) in length served as a sign of wealth and high status, being stored suspended from the roof in chiefs' houses. With its association with the gods, bundles of tapa were also kept in the houses dedicated to the gods of Tahiti, along with the divine images.

Today, little remains of the ancient art of tapa-making of Tahiti. By the early 1790s, imported cotton cloth was already beginning to replace it, and by the 1840s Tahitian tapa was a thing of the past. Contemporary Tahitian artists and scholars are now showing an increasing interest in reviving the knowledge and skills of traditional Tahitian tapa.

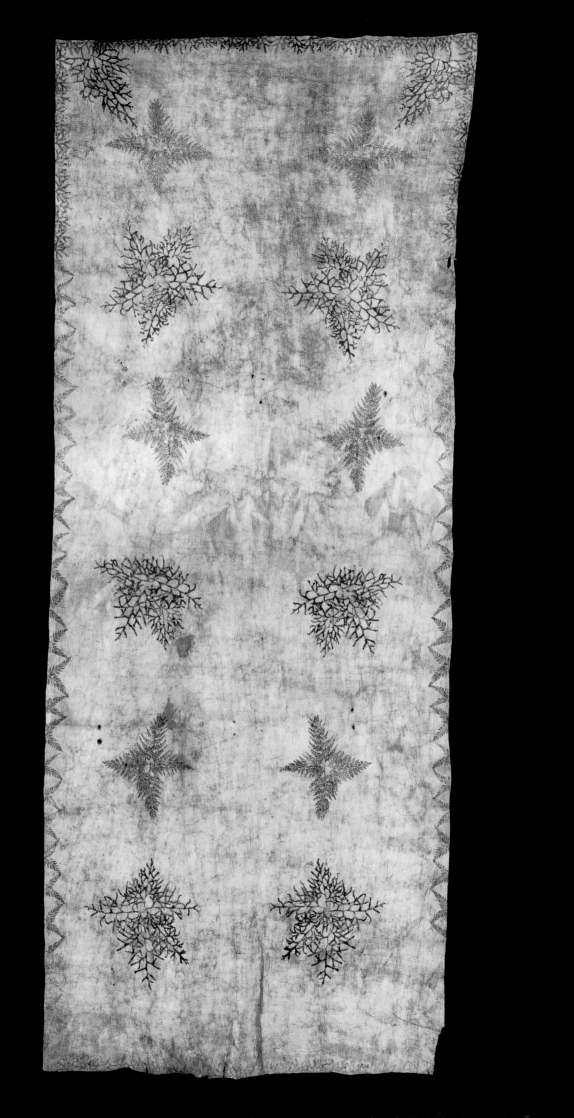

CHAPTER 10

NEW ZEALAND

Most people have now forgotten that the Maori of New Zealand made tapa, or *aute*, as both the paper mulberry tree and the finished cloth are called in Maori. The knowledge and skills for making barkcloth, and the paper mulberry tree itself, were introduced to New Zealand by the Polynesian ancestors of the Maori, probably about one thousand years ago. Since the paper mulberry does not set seeds in tropical Polynesia, these voyagers must have purposely brought carefully tended cuttings with them in their migration canoes, traditionally in the *Oturereao*, the *Aotea* and the *Tainui* canoes, on the long ocean voyage from Eastern Polynesia. The tree was cultivated in New Zealand throughout all the years of Maori history and survived the first years of European contact until the 1840s, when neglect of the plantations and browsing cattle brought about its extinction.

Aute, referred to in many of the ancient Maori oral histories, is described as a wrapping for the images of gods and other valuables, as a material for clothing before flax fibre-weaving techniques developed, as covering for kites, and as personal adornment used for items such as ornamental streamers and rolls worn in the hair and ears. The famous ancestor Kahungunu decorated his topknot of hair and his ear with *aute* cloth when embarking on an important journey in North Auckland. References to *maro aute*, aprons or girdles made of barkcloth, occur in stories about famous mythological and legendary women such as Taranga, the mother of Maui, and Hinepoupou, who swam across Cook Strait to follow her husband. Similarly, when Tawhaki climbed to heaven on the string of his kite, the material of his kite is described as *aute*. Many tribal proverbs mention *aute* as a common component of Maori material culture, especially in the North Auckland, Auckland, Waikato and Hauraki areas, indicating those parts of the country where *aute* was most common.

By the time the British and French explorers reached New Zealand in the late eighteenth century, the only remaining Maori use of tapa seen by them was as decorative rolls in men's perforated earlobes. The ornaments consisted of very small pieces of white tapa rolled and thrust through the hole, often with a greenstone ear pendant hanging below. At first, Maori men were very keen to trade for the larger pieces of white Tahitian tapa offered by the Europeans, but they soon lost interest when they realised that it was the same material as their *aute*. In the Bay of Islands in 1769, Cook and Banks were shown a small plantation of *aute* trees, obviously highly valued.

If these first European explorers collected any New Zealand *aute* cloth, it has not survived in any of the museum collections of early-contact Maori artefacts. Consequently, the best records that we have of the appearance of pre-European Maori tapa are the drawings made by early visiting artists, such as Sydney Parkinson with Captain Cook at Anaura Bay and Queen Charlotte Sound in 1769-70 and Augustus Earle in North Auckland in 1827-8. These show a white, unpigmented tapa, probably fairly thick and stiff, made only in very small pieces.

Paoi, tapa beaters, New Zealand. Made from local kauri branchwood, these New Zealand Maori tapa beaters, with their quadrangular grooved cross-sections, have been recovered from swamps and estuarine deposits. They provide firm material evidence of the manufacture of tapa in pre-European New Zealand.
Lengths from left: 31.4 cm, 31.4 cm, 34.9 cm.

Old tapa cloth has been found in some dry caves in inland Otago, in the South Island, most notably the pieces wrapped around and lining a *wakahuia*, treasure box, containing seventy *huia* (a bird now extinct) feathers hidden in a rock cleft on the Clutha River. Some of these pieces of Otago barkcloth might have been made from the bark of other trees, such as lacebark and ribbonwood, while others may be paper mulberry tapa brought to New Zealand from the tropical Pacific by early post-European travellers. In view of these doubtful origins, the Otago barkcloth finds are inconclusive evidence for the appearance of authentic New Zealand tapa.

The only material evidence for the manufacture of tapa in New Zealand are the fourteen known Maori *aute* beaters that have been found in swamps and coastal mud in North Auckland, Auckland, Waikato, Bay of Plenty and Taranaki, all made from native timbers such as kauri, rimu and *matai*. In basic form, with their longitudinal grooves and squared or triangular cross-sections, these New Zealand *aute* beaters are very similar to nineteenth-century tropical East Polynesian tapa beaters, but the New Zealand forms are more diverse than the beaters of any one tropical island group. This diversity may reflect different Pacific Island origins for New Zealand *aute* technology or may be the result of regional and tribal differentiation in tapa manufacture within the larger area of New Zealand during a thousand years of indigenous development.

Some of these New Zealand beaters are probably several hundred years old and are therefore among the oldest Polynesian tapa beaters in existence. The only other ancient Polynesian tapa beaters are those found in the Vaito'otia/Fa'ahia archaeological site on Huahine in French Polynesia, which dates from the ninth to the twelfth centuries AD. However, the Huahine beaters with their round cross-sections are fundamentally different from all the Maori *aute* beaters. Therefore, this difference does not support claims made for direct links between this early Huahine Polynesian culture and early Maori culture.

CHAPTER 11

HAWAII

In old Hawaii, tapa production and decoration reached a level of refinement and variety unsurpassed in any other culture of the Pacific. Unfortunately, Hawaiian culture also suffered greatly from the early impact of European penetration so that by the later nineteenth century the art of Hawaiian tapa-making had become extinct. Consequently, most Hawaiian tapa is now only found in earlier museum collections, and information on the tapa process in Hawaii is sketchy and incomplete. Auckland Museum is fortunate to possess a few pieces of Hawaiian tapa, along with some small samples in the museum's copy of Alexander Shaw's book of tapa collected on Captain Cook's voyages. Published in 1787 and now a very rare book, Shaw's catalogue is illustrated with actual small pieces of tapa, usually numbering about forty in each volume with the majority being from Tahiti and Hawaii.

Tapa, or *kapa* as it is called in Hawaiian, was made mainly from the bark of the paper mulberry, or *wauke*, which was cultivated especially for this purpose. Another important source of bark was the *mamaki* (*Pipturus albidus*) which grew wild and produced a coarser cloth. As in most of Polynesia, tapa in Hawaii was traditionally used mainly for clothing and sleeping coverings. Women's wrap-around skirts called *pa'u* were made of layers of tapa – sometimes as many as ten layers which could be several metres long. Men wore a tapa loincloth or *malo* which was a long narrow garment folded lengthwise to show designs on both sides. Both men and women occasionally wore a shoulder cape of tapa called a *kihei*, sometimes for warmth and sometimes for ceremonial decoration. *Kapa moe* or sleeping coverings were made of several layers of cloth sewn together and beautifully decorated on the upper layer. Other uses of tapa cloth included swaddling of newborn babies and wrapping the bones of the dead for burial. For religious rituals, images of the gods were dressed in fine white tapa and towers covered with tapa were erected in the temple grounds as places for the gods to enter.

Hawaii is one of the very few areas in the Pacific where a stone anvil was used for the first beating of the cloth with a round-sectioned beater. This produced long wide strips which were then soaked in water and allowed to ferment slightly to soften the fibres. A second beating with square-sectioned beaters macerated the fibres and enabled the layered strips to be felted into larger rectangular sheets. Sometimes, especially in the nineteenth century, while the cloth was still wet, elaborate geometric patterns carved into some of the beater facets were then repeatedly impressed on to the cloth, leaving a distinctive watermark pattern on the surface. Another technique which imparted a grooved or ribbed texture to the cloth was carried out by men who pressed the dampened cloth into parallel grooves cut into a special wooden board. Another distinctive Hawaiian practice was the application of pleasant smelling scent to tapa, included either during the manufacturing process or by adding it to the finished cloth.

Hawaii's wide range of plants provided many different coloured dyes (along with red and yellow ochres) for decorating tapa. As well as freehand painting, local experts

Opposite: *Kapa,* Hawaii. This very thin fine piece of watermarked barkcloth has coloured linear designs that have been applied by using bamboo printing stamps dipped into dye. This example probably dates from the early nineteenth century. 30 x 25 cm.

Left: *Kapa,* Hawaii. Collected in 1812, this small torn piece has a fine pattern ruled on to the cloth with wooden-pronged liners dipped into the pigment. 38 × 17 cm.

Opposite: *Kapa,* Hawaii. A selection of actual pieces of Hawaiian tapa cloth from the Auckland Museum's copy of Alexander Shaw's book of tapa collected on Captain Cook's voyages, published in 1787. The patterns include bold angular freehand designs prevalent in eighteenth-century Hawaiian tapa, and also some of the finer ruled designs that became more popular later.

displayed great ingenuity in developing multi-pronged liners, fine pens and thin-patterned bamboo printing stamps for applying these colours in abstract geometric and asymmetrical patterns. Eighteenth-century Hawaiian tapa is relatively thick, often grooved, and features bold angular designs. Nineteenth-century tapa is finer and thinner, often watermarked, and decorated with intricate, elaborate, repeated printed designs.

Imported blankets and woven textiles for clothing soon replaced tapa in Hawaii, although production of less functional elaborately patterned fine tapa for gift-giving and ceremonial purposes continued a little longer. Now, after nearly a century of extinction, Hawaiian tapa-making has been revived by dedicated Hawaiian crafts-women who have re-learnt aspects of the manufacturing process from Tongan, Samoan and Fijian experts, supplemented by study of old Hawaiian tapa in museum collections and their own experimentation.

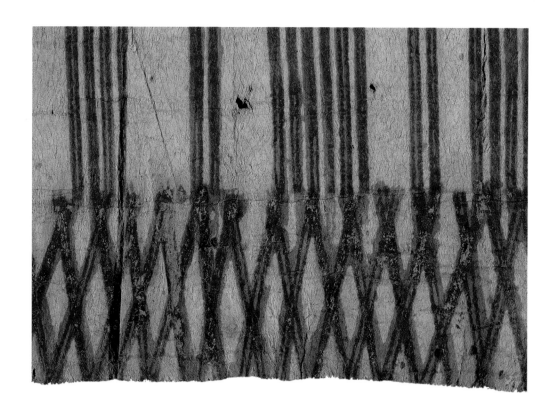

Opposite: *Kapa*. Hawaii. Probably made as a man's loincloth, or *malo*, this cloth has been ornamented with coloured lines applied by a wooden-pronged liner drawn along a ruler. Details of this tapa are shown above and below. The detail below shows the original stitching on the rear of the garment. 242 x 64 cm.

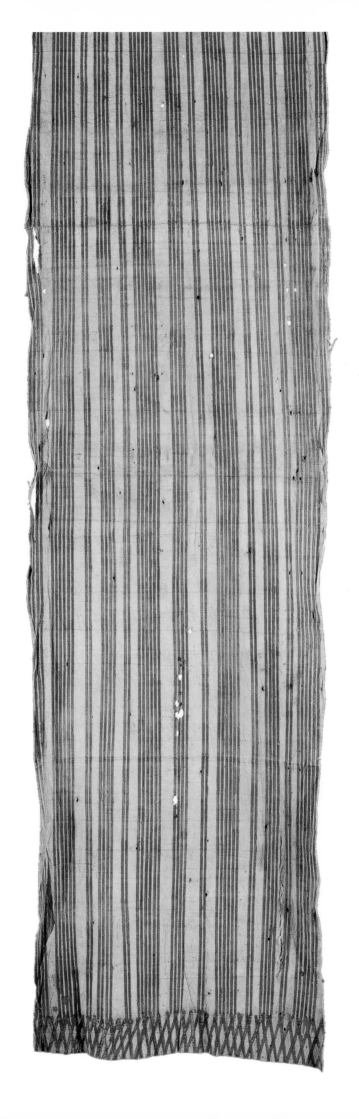

FIJI

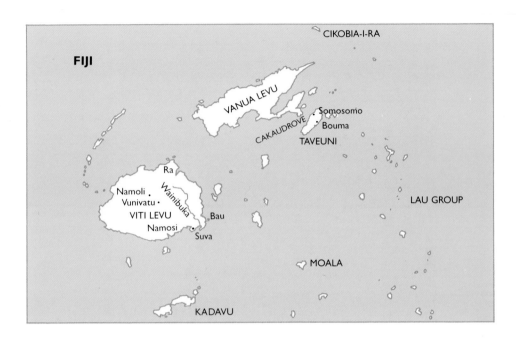

The tapa of Fiji, generally known as *masi*, is made almost without exception from the inner bark of paper mulberry. Most of the cloth used traditionally was white and known as *masi vulavula*. Some districts such as Ra became famous for their white cloth – producing no other and trading it over a wide area. Patterned *masi* was also produced but its prominence in museum collections is mainly due to the enthusiasm shown by European collectors for ornamentation. Nevertheless, the people of Fiji have probably used more tapa decoration techniques than any other Pacific group.

The most popular style at the present time is *masi kesa*, a white cloth decorated with black and brown stencilled patterns. Each motif is cut out from a piece of banana or other large leaf and the pigment is rubbed through the opening with a wad of tapa. If X-ray film is available it is now used in preference to leaf as it makes a stronger and longer lasting stencil. In the normal procedure, a pattern is first applied around the edge of the cloth using one or more small stencils which are repeated to form a border. Working inward from the outer edge, further bands are added. If a large space is left in the centre it may be filled with larger motifs. Stencils were also used for another type of pattern in which small black motifs were widely spaced across a plain white surface. These cloths sometimes have border patterns as well.

Perhaps the most striking of all the Fijian patterns are the bold black and white rectilinear and diagonal patterns produced in the Cakaudrove area, which includes Taveuni and the south coast of Vanua Levu. To set out the pattern, the cloth is first carefully folded, concertina style, with each fold representing the edge of a painted area. Black pigment is rubbed on the edges of the folds so that when the cloth is opened out parts of the pattern are neatly outlined. Subsequent foldings add to the complexity of the pattern. The black areas are then painted in using a section of a

Left: Design rollers, 1910s, Namoli, central Viti Levu, Fiji. The man on the left holds a variant on the *bitu ni kesakesa* design roller, but in this case made from a very solid tree trunk rather than bamboo. With its alternating wide and narrow grooves, this would be called a *noa* in the local dialect. The man on the right holds a small roller of bamboo which would be called a *lewasanga* locally because of its very fine narrow grooves. These rollers were used by men to apply a sombre dark pattern to the tapa produced in the highlands of Viti Levu.

Opposite: *Masi kesa*, Fiji. Decorating a tapa with cut-out stencils is a Fijian technique that is not used elsewhere. To apply small black motifs, the stencil is placed on the cloth and pressed with a small pigmented wad of tapa. Sometimes, the motifs are widely spaced, as on the central panel in this example; at other times the stencil motif is repeated over and over again to form more complex designs, such as the cross-bands and border on this cloth. 212 x 74 cm.

pandanus fruit as a brush. A strip of leaf laid on top can be used to shield the white areas and a stencil may be used for other areas. Narrow stencilled bands of fine brown patterns add a finishing touch. Large cloths of this type were folded so that the pattern was visible from both sides and used to screen the bride and groom during wedding ceremonies. Long narrow tapa strips in "Cakaudrove style" were worn as belts and scarves over other tapa clothing.

In the eastern areas, particularly in the Lau group where Tongan influence is strong, Tongan-type rubbing blocks are used. The tapa is laid on top of the tablet and a pigmented wad of cloth rubbed over it in the same way that a rubbing may be taken from a coin with a pencil. The block is made from short lengths of coconut leaflets, arranged and sewn into place on a wad of pandanus leaves or palm spathe. Large cloths patterned from these are still called *gatu vakatoga*, which translates as "Tongan cloth made in the Tongan way". For ceremonial presentation they are spread out and carried by a large number of women.

In Fiji a number of types of rubbing tablets developed. Some were carved on to a flat board similar to those still used in Samoa. Others were built up from strips of bamboo bound on to the convex surface of a log. Sombre dark tapa, from the highlands west of the main divide of Viti Levu, was made by rubbing black and brown pigment on a tapa arranged over a length of bamboo with parallel grooves incised around it, known as *bitu ni kesakesa*. There were three types: one with wide grooves and ridges, one with narrow grooves and ridges, and one with alternating groups of wide and narrow grooves and ridges. When the bamboo with the fine

Warrior in full costume, 1880s, Fiji. Well armed with short throwing clubs and a long two-handed club, this warrior wears a necklace cut from sperm whale teeth and a *malo* loincloth painted with bold freehand patterns.

Women in tapa clothing, 1900s, Fiji. With their hair in traditional short style, these women pose in tapa clothing consisting of Cakaudrove-style strips wrapped around their upper bodies and a skirt of stencilled *masi kesa*.

ridging is used, the patterning is so intense that some parts may appear to be plain black or brown until it is held to the light when the subtle variation of colour and pattern can be seen. This cloth was made by women but decorated by men. On Kadavu Island a heavy tapa is recorded as being made by men, but this is unusual in Fiji, where *masi* is normally made and decorated by women.

In the Lau Group, *gatu vakaviti* is a class of tapa that developed locally, and combines the rubbed patterns introduced from Tonga with Fijian stencilled technique. *Gatu vakaviti* may be translated as "Tongan cloth in the style of Fiji".

Fiji was also famous for fine cloth made from a single thickness of immature paper mulberry. Veil-like and translucent, it floated like a long train behind a chief of great importance. It could be pure white, or by carefully smoking it over a frame of saplings, deep brown, lightened by paler orange lines where the saplings shielded the tapa from the smoke. Brilliant orange-yellow cloth was obtained by dyeing in turmeric. These delicate cloths were sometimes further decorated by folding them concertina style, which caused them to flutter in the slightest breeze.

One more method used in Fiji was shared with Samoa. The technique involved painting the cloth freehand, often with a brush made from a section of a pandanus fruit. Finer lines were applied with a bamboo pen. The decoration could be restrained with delicate motifs widely spaced across a white ground. Fine lines and lettering were also used at times, the latter sometimes helping with the identification of unlocalised pieces. Other hand-painted patterns were more complex, covering the entire surface and often repeating the motifs on a grid. A feature of patterns made in this manner is that there are frequently breaks in the repetition which provide visual

Sisi, Vanua Levu, Fiji. Whale ivory is highly valued in Fiji. It is inlaid on wooden clubs and headrests, split and shaped into long narrow tusks arranged as neck ornaments, and cut into large round breastplates. Large individual whales' teeth, *tabua*, are important in ceremonial exchanges and are highly valued, especially if they have an ancient golden patina. The *sisi* necklace illustrated is made of complete whales' teeth threaded on coconut coir and held in position with a wrapping of tapa. *Tabua* have retained their cultural value and are still presented as ceremonial gifts, to ask for a favour, or to apologise for an offence. Length of largest tooth 9.2 cm.

variety. When these changes are minor, the viewer may not be consciously aware of their presence, but the formality is softened by the changes. Obvious changes in the pattern may appear to be mistakes but we cannot be sure that this is always the case. In some instances, they appear to be quite intentional. At other times, it seems that a number of people have been working together, some with a steadier hand than others, and some who have perhaps misunderstood the motif. Sometimes it is possible to pick out the work of an apparent individual by thicker lines or some other mannerism. Whatever the case, it is rare for these variations or errors to detract from the impact of the completed work – and in fact they often add to its appeal.

This wide variety of methods of tapa decoration in Fiji may reflect the complexity of the population. It is here that Melanesia and Polynesia merge and Fijian culture has been influenced from both directions. The earliest settlers arrived from Melanesia more than three thousand years ago. Some of them settled, while others moved on into Polynesia. Later, there were backward movements from Polynesia and subsequent migrations from Melanesia. This resulted in a checkerboard of cultures, with some retaining parts of their own distinct traditions, and others absorbing or being absorbed into earlier groups.

By the beginning of the nineteenth century, when European influence was first beginning to be felt in the area, large indigenous ocean-going vessels frequented the waters between Fiji, Tonga and Samoa. They carried warriors set on conquest for their chiefs or fighting as mercenaries for others. Canoe builders sought large trees for timber, or were employed in their trade by foreign chiefs. Red feathers, fine mats and tapa were among the trade goods carried.

Craftsmen and women carried their skills with them and sometimes settled. Among these were a large number of Tongans who settled the eastern parts of Fiji, particularly in the Lau Group between Fiji and Tonga. Although Lau is politically part of Fiji, the influence of western Polynesia is still strong and evident in the language, culture and appearance of the people.

Traditionally, Fijian men wore the *malo*, a breechclout of tapa between 3 and 6 metres (10 and 20 feet) long. It passed between the legs and several times around the body. For important men and on dress occasions the *malo* could be up to a 100 metres (328 feet) long. The end in front hung down to the knees, while the other end was tied up in a bunch or allowed to trail behind. A sash was tied higher around the body and the ends allowed to fall as trains. The large, carefully groomed hairstyles of the men were wrapped in a sheet of very fine tapa known as *isala*. Women, on the other hand, were forbidden to use tapa and their dress consisted of a short, fringed sash of dyed plant fibre called a *liku*.

Both male and female styles of dress greatly offended the early missionaries who imposed the wearing of cloth wrap-arounds as a minimum. Their demands must have been intimidating as in 1862 Eduard Graeffe, a visiting Swiss naturalist, reported that men unable to obtain cotton cloth had to make do with wearing the female *liku* over the *malo* – surely embarrassing to say the least, in such a male-dominated society.

The most important uses of tapa in Fiji were for gifts, trade and tributes. There are still occasions in Fiji where large amounts of tapa change hands, particularly at weddings and funerals. The amounts of tapa and the ritual involved can seem quite astounding to outsiders unfamiliar with the customs, but amazing as they are, these modern ceremonies pale beside those recorded in the past.

Graeffe described a presentation of tapa made to the chief of the mountain village of Vunivatu by three Namosi chiefs who accompanied him. The Namosi chiefs dressed themselves for the meeting by painting their faces and upper bodies and wrapping a huge amount of tapa around their waists "making their trunks look enormous". When they approached their host they unrolled the tapa by rotating their bodies until they wore only their *malo*, and then proceeded to present the tapa and also *tabua*, whales' teeth, which they had concealed in the folds of their tapa.

At a presentation from the people of Somosomo to the chiefs of Bau in 1858 more than twenty large bales of cloth were brought out, one by one, and were laid down amid shouts and the blowing of trumpet shells. Each of these bales were 4 to 6 metres (15 to 20 feet) long and took many men to carry it. Soon Ratu Vaalolo, the son of the chief of Somosomo, appeared under a load of stained cloth, hanging in folds from his shoulders to his knees, and followed by a train of tapa 20 fathoms

· Above: *Kuveji*, rubbing board, Fiji. Made from a discarded wooden door, this rubbing board for imprinting a tapa design incorporates the date of 1892 and other text into the pattern. The language of the text suggests that it may have come from an area of Fiji with a strong Polynesian influence. 74 × 43 cm.

Ceremonial presentation of gifts, 1953, Fiji. Young women dressed in tapa skirts over cotton *lavalava* parade rolls of plaited mats which are being presented to Queen Elizabeth II.

Masi kuvui, smoked tapa, Fiji. Smoked *masi* is made by soaking finely beaten cloth in coconut oil and then spreading it over a wood frame under which a smoky fire is ignited. The cloth is stained an orange-brown with lighter areas of yellow and a dull sheen on the surface. It was once used only by priests and chiefs, and is now reserved for important ceremonial occasions. Left: 169 × 44 cm. Middle: 205 × 88 cm. Right: 534 × 50 cm.

(36 metres, or 120 feet) long. This he threw down in front of the Bau chiefs and returned to repeat the act five times. Each time he threw down the cloth the warriors shouted. Ratu Vaalolo and O Mai Tavui then rushed twice into the open space twirling their fans before Ratu na Vu appeared among loud shouts. His train was 90 metres (300 feet) long and he was followed by 200 men with large *masi* hung from their shoulders. Next came two men carrying a long pole with four large *masi* tied up and hung on it. These were followed by one 100 men with large *masi* who seated themselves near the bales, where they were joined by another 250 similarly attired men who approached from another entrance.

The importance of tapa also extended to religion. The only way to obtain access to the influence of the gods was through the medium of the priest. A long piece of white cloth, suspended from the beam of the temple house, hung down so that the end lay on the floor in front of the corner post. When summoned, it was down this path that the god passed to enter the priest and commune with him.

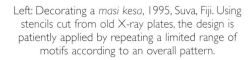

Left: Decorating a *masi kesa*, 1995, Suva, Fiji. Using stencils cut from old X-ray plates, the design is patiently applied by repeating a limited range of motifs according to an overall pattern.

Below left: *Meke* dance with fans and bamboos, 1870s, Wainibuka, Viti Levu, Fiji. With shell and ivory breastplates, their faces blackened with charcoal and their bodies coated in coconut oil, these warriors wear a variety of tapa clothing. Long white cloths around their waists are draped over freehand-painted wrap-arounds and their heads are covered with white and brown tapa turbans.

Opposite: *Masi vulavula*, Fiji. (Left) In old Fiji, particular care was taken in the production of fine white tapa known as *masi vulavula* which was carefully beaten out to muslin-like fineness to be worn by men as turbans, sashes and scarves. During beating, small twig holes were covered by pulling one edge of the hole across to the other and so creating a triangular patch. These were seen as a decorative element and were then created even where there was no hole. 216 x 75 cm. (Right) Another form of *masi vulavula* is *masi vakadrau*, on which the decoration is described as *vakadrau*, meaning "leaf-like". The edges of joins or added patches are allowed to hang free as a filmy fringe. 351 x 44 cm.

As living standards and expectations of villagers have changed over the years, a need for a cash income has developed. Trade goods such as clothing, canned food, rice, petrol and kerosene have all become necessities even in more remote areas. An influx of tourists from the 1960s created a demand for souvenirs and the Fijians responded with an increase in the production of *masi*. Being light and easy to pack, as well as an exotic and attractive memento of the South Seas, it was soon in great demand. Smaller pieces that could be displayed on a table or wall were made to suit the tastes of visitors. The tapa-makers have found that they are able to produce and sell these individually and this has brought about a departure from the traditional situation where a large number of women worked together to produce large quantities of cloth for community use.

Production for the tourist market continues today but *masi* is still manufactured for traditional purposes as well. Areas without a tapa-making tradition obtain what they require through traditional exchange systems by supplying their own specialities, such as plaited pandanus mats, in exchange.

Right: Pattern stencil, Lau, Fiji. An original type of stencil for applying black dye patterns to *masi kesa*, cut in a banana leaf. Most stencils are now cut from disused X-ray plates. 21 cm long.

Above: *Bitu ni kesakesa*, bamboo rollers, Highlands of Viti Levu, Fiji. With their grooves cut into a length of bamboo, these rollers are used to apply a pattern to the sombre dark tapa made in the mountain districts of Viti Levu. In the local mountain dialect of Fijian, rollers with medium-spaced grooves were known as *baba*. (Top) 89 cm long × 7 cm diameter; (Bottom) 83 cm long × 7 cm diameter.

Above: *Ike*, tapa beater, Fiji. Fiji is one of the few areas in the Pacific where some tapa beaters have a three-sided triangular cross-section, like this rare example. 37.3 cm long.

Below: *Ike*, tapa beater, Fiji. Fijian tapa beaters with an oval cross-section are characteristic of the highlands of central Viti Levu, where they probably derive from an older Melanesian cultural expression. 36.5 cm long.

Above: *Ike*, tapa beaters, Fiji. A selection of Fijian tapa beaters with rectangular cross-sections is displayed here. A wide range of beater types is used in various parts of the Fijian archipelago, probably reflecting diverse Polynesian and Melanesian influences. (Left) 29.3 cm long, (Middle) 37 cm long, (Right) 41.5 cm long.

Masi kesa, Taveuni Island, Cakaudrove district, Fiji. This stencil-patterned *masi kesa* has two fringed and two serrated edges. 207 × 159 cm.

Following spread: Fijian tapa decorative motifs.

Above: *Masi,* Fiji. A single stencil was used to decorate the whole of this piece of fine white tapa. 267 × 103 cm.

Opposite: *Masi bolabola,* Cakaudrove district, Fiji. Tapa from some parts of Fiji can readily be identified by the arrangement and colour of the motifs. The striking black and white patterns on the tapa of the Cakaudrove area is mostly hand-painted. (Left) 389 × 57 cm, (Middle) 674 × 60 cm, (Right) 353 × 64 cm.

Above: *Gatu vakatoga,* Fiji. This cloth has been patterned from a rubbing block made by sewing an arrangement of strips of pandanus leaf and coconut leaflet midribs on to a wad of coconut leaf sheath. This is the method used today in Tonga, but it has also been used in Fiji and Samoa, probably after introduction from Tonga. The unusual selection and fine painting of the triangular shapes suggests this piece may be of Fijian origin. 248 × 100 cm.

Right: *Masi*, Probably Lau Islands, Fiji. The Tongan-style rubbed patterns on the brown squares suggest this cloth is from one of the Tongan-influenced islands in the Lau group. 156 x 131 cm.

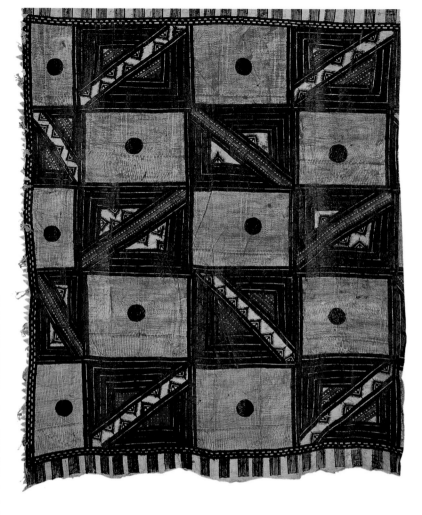

Opposite: *Masi*, Fiji or Samoa. An unusual pattern combining carefully drawn freehand rectilinear motifs with curving lines, painted entirely in black. 221 x 93 cm.

Left: *Masi bolabola*, Cakaudrove district, Fiji. This example contains an outlined pattern painted black on a white background with small stencilled motifs in brown. 670 x 117 cm.

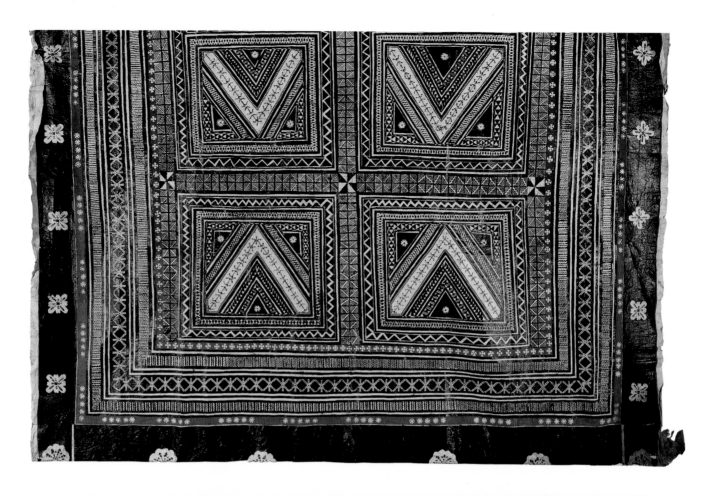

Right: *Masi,* Fiji. Repetition is avoided in this arresting pattern of repeating triangles by placing them in a striking asymmetrical arrangement. 358 × 64 cm.

Opposite: *Taunamu,* Bouma village, Taveuni Island, Fiji. The photographs show the two halves of a large cloth. This large stencilled *taunamu* was made on the order of the Tui Cakau by the women of Bouma, the village named on the cloth. It was ceremonially presented to Lady Lala Mara, the wife of the then Prime Minister of Fiji, at a meeting of the Great Council of Chiefs in about 1985. 550 × 410 cm.

Following pages: *Taunamu,* probably Moala Island, Fiji. A large and very striking stencilled cloth, probably a *taunamu* intended to be suspended over a cord as a house-divider and/or a mosquito guard. The name "*taunamu*" refers to the function of these cloths in keeping mosquitoes out of the house. 373 × 412 cm.

CHAPTER 13

VANUATU

Tapa-making was not widespread in the islands of Vanuatu, which are more famous for the fineness of their openwork plaited mats. According to early European voyagers and missionaries, tapa was produced only on Efate and the small islands of Nguna, Tongoa and Emae just to the north of Efate, and on Tanna, Aneityum and Eromanga in southern Vanuatu. Some ethnologists have argued that these are areas which have been influenced by Polynesian culture in the ancient past.

By the early years of this century, the only tapa items being made in Vanuatu were the rudimentary tapa belts worn by the men of Tanna and Eromanga. These belts of coarse tapa were about 5 cm (2 in) wide and up to 2 metres (6 feet 6 in) long, worn folded to form a shorter strip of cloth that was often painted with simple stripes. This belt then held up a penis wrapper.

In former times, women's clothing in Efate consisted of tapa loincloths produced on Nguna, Tongoa and Emae and on Efate itself. This tapa was painted brown and yellow, mostly in geometric patterns, with the lower edges of the loincloths decorated in feathers. The manufacture of these loincloths had ceased by about the middle of the nineteenth century and only rare examples survive in a few museum collections.

Eromanga was the other main centre of tapa production in Vanuatu and most of the Vanuatu tapa now in museum collections has come from this island. Some early tapa beaters from Eromanga were elaborately carved on their beating facets to impress herringbone designs into the tapa. Later nineteenth-century beaters were plain and often quite roughly finished. Nevertheless, Eromanga was once well known for its handsome painted tapa used for women's upper garments worn across the shoulders over a full trailing skirt of plaited pandanus strips. Sometimes, especially while she was working in the gardens, a mother would carry her sleeping baby in her tapa garment made into a sling.

Tapa on Eromanga is known as *nemasitse*, meaning simply beaten cloth. It was made only by women, from the inner bark of the banyan and certain other large trees. Strips of bark were cut from the tree and beaten on a large wooden anvil while water was sprayed on to the pulpy bark. Overlapping strips of bark were added in and beaten to felt them together, until the desired width was reached. When beating was finished, the sheet of dull white cloth was hung over creepers or bamboo, and while still damp, the patterns were drawn on with a piece of charcoal. Favourite designs are said to be based on the crescent moon, birds, fishes, flying foxes, various leaves and simple human figures. The sheet was then left to dry completely before it was dyed by being dipped into a solution coloured with tree-root scrapings. This dye provided a reddish-yellow colour which was only taken up by the areas marked in charcoal, leaving the rest of the cloth in its natural colour. Alternatively, the whole cloth might be dyed a yellowish-brown by lengthy immersion in a special mud. Towards the end of the nineteenth century some transitional designs depicting men on horses and other introduced objects, began to appear but this innovation had little time to

Opposite: Tapa, Eromanga, Vanuatu. Although the locality of this tapa was not recorded, it is thought to be from Eromanga because of its similarity to known Eromanga tapa. Tapa was made in several scattered places in Vanuatu, but usually in small pieces for belts and loincloths. Only on Eromanga were larger freehand decorated sheets of tapa produced, from the bark of the banyan tree. 73 x 60 cm.

develop before the art of tapa-making itself became extinct.

Tapa production on Eromanga had ceased by the turn of the century but the knowledge and techniques of its manufacture were retained by some older people. For a brief period when the beginning of World War II disrupted shipping in the Pacific, the Eromanga people temporarily revived tapa-making to compensate for the shortage of imported cloth. This shortage was soon remedied by the arrival of American soldiers who gave away clothing to the islanders. But as a result of this brief revival, a new younger generation of Eromanga people learnt how to make tapa – even though production was only short-lived. By the 1980s, this generation had reached an old age but they were still able to instruct a young Eromanga man in the local art of tapa manufacture, thereby perhaps saving the art for the future.

CHAPTER 14

TIKOPIA

Tikopia, a tiny island outlier of Polynesian culture to the east of the Solomon Islands, is one of the increasingly rare Polynesian communities where barkcloth may still be seen in use as everyday clothing. There are no shops on the island and, except for teachers and the medical officer, no cash incomes. Family members living in other parts of the Solomons sometimes send or bring goods home and cotton clothing is popular, with the newest items being reserved for churchgoing. Men, particularly young men, often prefer shorts to the traditional *maro,* citing the rough, abrasive quality of barkcloth as the main reason. However, it is not uncommon to see adults, both male and female, in traditional attire. The women wear a wrap-around barkcloth skirt called *raroa* while men wear a barkcloth breechclout or *maro,* usually beneath a commercial cotton wrap-around.

Children are also familiar with wearing barkcloth. For the two schools on the island, the school uniform is traditional tapa dress worn on set days each week and at other times if preferred or necessary. The intention is to keep the children familiar with tradition and to ensure that those without imported cotton clothing are not unusual.

The tree used for barkcloth is known locally as *te mami* (*Antiaris toxicaria*). The cloth it provides is much thicker and heavier than that of the paper mulberry (*Broussonetia*), although material from younger trees is thin. Tapa made from *te mami* is inclined to be stiff, at least until it has been worn for some time, but it is long lasting and strong, being used particularly by men when fishing from canoes. Sheets of *te mami* used to sleep on are often smooth and soft with a texture rather like chamois leather.

At festivals, barkcloth appears for the dance. It is never decorated with patterns, but instead is often stained bright orange with turmeric, particularly for important occasions. The arms and shoulders of the dancers may also be painted with turmeric.

The *maro* is a true breechclout. It is put on by holding the wider end of the cloth over the chest and against the genitals. The remaining long narrowing section is passed back between the legs, and then up behind, and around the waist to hold the upright front-covering in place. This flap is now lowered and the remainder of the long strip wrapped round the waist a number of times, passing over the flap and holding it in place. The narrow tail end is then looped though the first round at the back, just above the cleavage, and the garment is secure. On more formal occasions, and in the company of an *ariki* or other important persons, and when posing for photographs, the flap is spread more widely and worn very much longer, almost to the ankles in some cases. The width of the entire cloth is also wider for these occasions.

The woman's skirt, *raroa,* is a simple rectangle of cloth large enough to reach around the body and overlap in front. Worn by girls and young women, it may reach to just below the knees but is worn longer by married and older women. It is held in place with a sash of tapa or a multiple cord belt of red braided coconut coir.

Below: Schoolgirls dancing, 1977, Tikopia. Schoolgirls from Terano school dancing at a church festival. They are wearing their school uniform of traditional barkcloth skirts, some of which have been stained orange with turmeric.

Following pages: *Maro tafi*, Tikopia. A man's breechclout, stained orange with turmeric for wearing on festive occasions. Women wear a wrap-around tapa skirt which may also be dyed with turmeric. This *maro* was part of a ceremonial gift given to anthropologist Raymond Firth at the *pungaumu*, initiation, of J. Munakina in 1928, when Firth was gathering information for his famous book, *We, the Tikopia. Maro tafi* were also used as offerings to the gods. 467 × 47 cm.

Above: Family in tapa clothing, 1973, Tikopia. Pa Rangifuri and his wife and family have dressed in their best clothes for the photo and all are wearing tapa cloth. Nau Rangifuri and daughter Rose Nuanga are wearing barkcloth skirts. Pa Rangifuri and sons John Karanga and Dunstan are dressed in traditional *maro*. When they have been stained orange with turmeric, as seen here, they are known as *maro tafi*. Pa Rangifuri also wears *te kie*, a prestigious plaited mat of pandanus leaf strips.

Gifts and payments usually include tapa. A common form, also known as *maro*, consists of a bundle of barkcloth and a mat. A typical gift *maro* contains a plaited pandanus sleeping mat, one or more barkcloth blankets, a couple of uncoloured *maro (maro tea)*, topped off with a turmeric-stained *maro tafi*. The gift is presented along with cooked and uncooked food.

Barkcloth features in the rites of passage. For the ceremony in which his foreskin is cut, a boy wears a new white *maro*, but immediately after the operation he is re-dressed in a prestigious, new, tumeric-dyed *maro tafi*. He is then carried to his father's house, greeted by his father's relatives and then rests on a great pile of pandanus mats and is covered with sheets of barkcloth – so many of them, that upright sticks are placed to keep the weight off him.

Similarly, barkcloth forms an important part of marriage exchanges and is included with fine mats in the payment that moves from the house of the bride to that of the groom. Wooden bowls, paddles and braided coir are the main items to move in the opposite direction to the house of the bride.

At the time of death, the body is dressed in barkcloth, painted with turmeric and then wrapped in mats and barkcloth to form a very large bundle for burial. Mourners often wear a strip of cloth that belonged to the deceased as a sign of mourning.

Before conversion to Christianity, tapa held an indispensable position in many religious activities. The prosperity of society, fertility of the gardens, success in fishing and gathering activities, and safety at sea all relied on offerings to the gods – of which barkcloth was a necessary component. Offerings including tapa assured the spiritual powers of the sacred chiefs, their rituals and their influence over the gods and ancestors. Without it the gods could not be influenced.

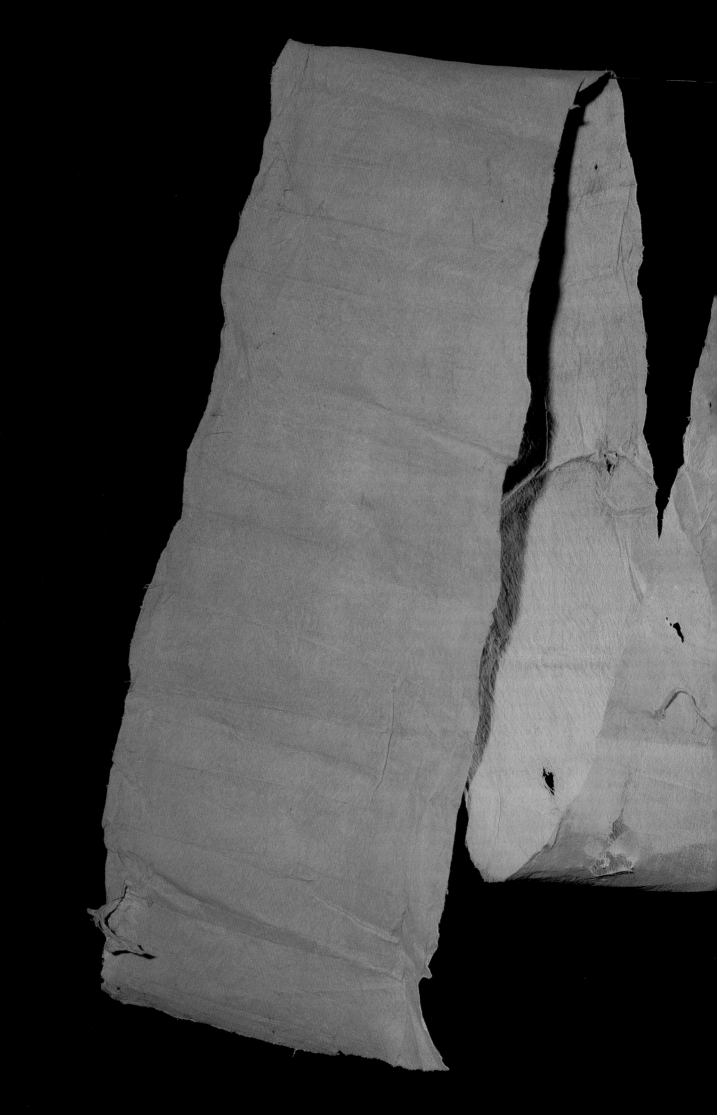

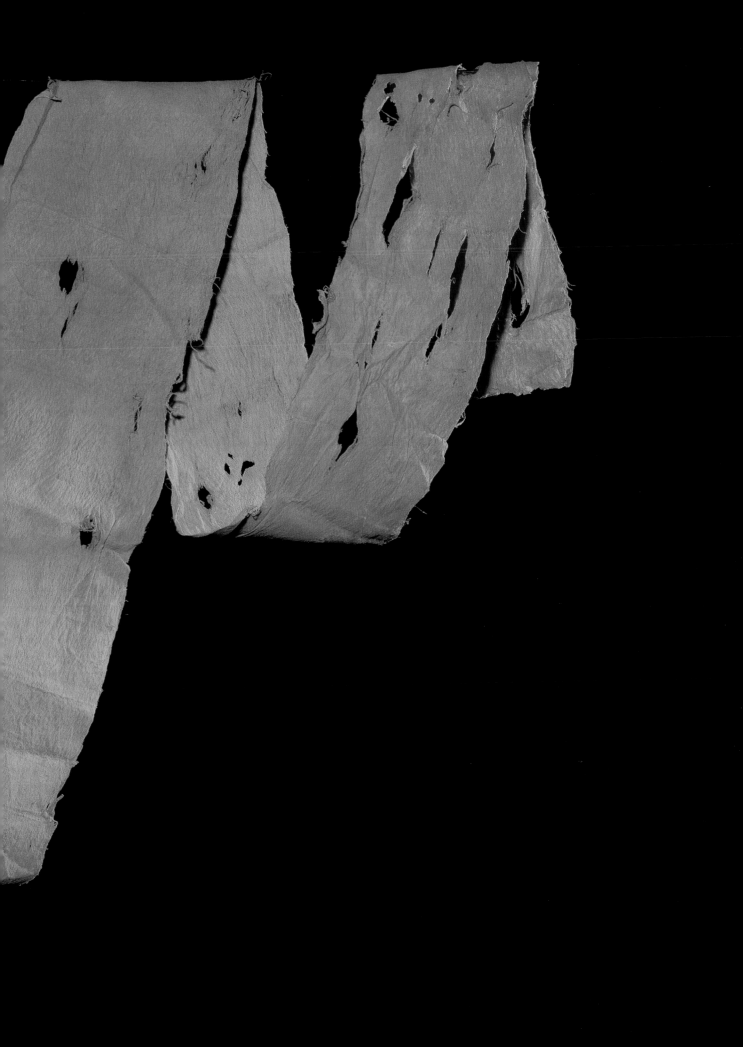

CHAPTER 15

SANTA CRUZ ISLANDS

The Santa Cruz Group consists of a small number of islands including Ndende, the central and largest island, which is often referred to as Santa Cruz. Although there are a number of languages, some of which are unrelated, a degree of mutual tolerance and understanding was reached through a complex trading system. Woven cloth, along with red feather money, shell valuables, timber and canoes, sennit cordage and wives, travelled on ocean-going canoes along the trading routes linking each island.

Ndende is one of the few areas in the Pacific where both weaving and tapa manufacture were practised. Fine breechclouts made on a back-loom were woven from tree bast. These were decorated at intervals with bands of patterns provided by the black fibre obtained by stripping the stems of a species of wild banana. Flat bags woven from the same materials were alternative male cover. Both were worn on special occasions, particularly when dance was involved, when they were stained with turmeric.

Less is known about the use and manufacture of the local tapa known as *lepau*. Early photographs show men wearing small apron-like coverings of barkcloth. Others show important men in costume with a tall cylinder of finely patterned tapa around the head. Tapa was made on Ndende Island and does not seem to have been documented for the other islands, although it is possible that some of the collected pieces and photographs recorded as being from Santa Cruz may in fact be from the outer islands.

Tapa had not been made since about the 1930s until the early 1970s, when a few school teachers were experimenting with its production in the hope of introducing the craft into school art programmes which were starved for art materials. The tree

Opposite: *Lepau*, Santa Cruz. Santa Cruz tapa is divided into rectangles which are decorated with fine black hatching. Old photographs show these cloths being worn as a cylindrical head-dress by important men. Tapa was also worn as a male breechclout, but for this purpose it was usually left undecorated. The bright orange colour of turmeric was ritually significant in Santa Cruz and was used on weapons, clothing and as body paint. Sometimes it was used to paint the borders in tapa patterns. The piece on the left was collected by the famous early missionary Rev. George Brown, at some time in the 1870s. 222 × 67 cm. The cloth on the right is 293 × 45 cm.

Right: Dancing party, 1906, Nelua village, Ndende, Santa Cruz Islands. This is a very rare photograph showing tapa being worn in Santa Cruz. Some of the men are wearing tapa breechclouts but others, including the leader in front, are wearing loom-woven pubic covers. On his head the leader wears a cylinder of patterned Santa Cruz tapa.

Above and opposite: Santa Cruz tapa decorative motifs.

used is *Antiaris toxicaria*, known locally in the area around Graciosa Bay as *nokali*. By the late 1980s a few pieces were reaching the commercial market in Honiara, the capital of the Solomons, and are still being produced today, but only intermittently.

In traditional work the cloth is divided into rectangles, each of which is filled with fine black patterns, usually involving cross-hatching. The margins between these areas of pattern may be painted orange with turmeric. In the recent revival, the new patterns are set out in the same manner, by dividing the cloth into rectangles and painting the margins with turmeric. However, the patterns within the rectangles are now filled with more widely spaced motifs, usually rectilinear and sometimes apparently naturalistic. Bird-like motifs are particularly evident. The patterns are quite unlike those on older cloths and may take their inspiration from those on painted local artefacts, such as dance clubs.

128

CHAPTER 16

SOLOMON ISLANDS

Right: Beating bast for tapa, c.1900s, Solomon Islands. A Solomon Islands woman beginning to beat out a piece of tapa on her cylindrical anvil. She is using a wooden beater with a round section which is typical of some areas in the Solomons.

Opposite: Tapa, probably New Georgia or Santa Isabel Islands, Solomon Islands. Women from some of the western islands in the Solomons wore breechclouts made from blue-dyed tapa cloth with a cushion-like padding behind. 177 x 136 cm.

The Solomon Islands are home to a range of diverse cultural groups. There are over sixty separate languages and a similar range of artforms. Tapa has been recorded mainly in the western islands of New Georgia and Santa Isabel. It was made from a number of trees, among the most common being *kalala* and *barekoto*, both species of banyan (*Ficus* spp.) which provide red/brown cloth. A white tapa made from another species was dyed blue with *pau* (wild indigo). The cloth may also be painted blue, spattered with blue or patterned with distinctive bold blue patterns sometimes depicting bird, shark or dugong motifs. It is said that the women of Santa Isabel were the experts in making the blue cloth and it was apparently traded to New Georgia.

Tapa was produced by methods similar to those used elsewhere: drying, soaking and beating were the basic processes. The beaters from the region are made from a dense black wood and are usually round in section with deep longitudinal grooves. Square-section beaters are found on Santa Isabel.

Men of the area wore a neat but brief breechclout of blue-dyed or natural-brown cloth. Old photographs show women wearing a similar but larger garment which is padded out at the back to form a large triangular cushion. This covering was too skimpy to please the early missionaries in New Georgia who encouraged the wearing of cotton cloth. Cotton clothing soon became the mark of a Christian convert, and eventually the wearing of tapa became unacceptable. Consequently, the art of making tapa was almost lost, but recent cultural festivals have encouraged Santa Isabel women to rediscover the unique blue tapa worn by their ancestors. Today, it is worn as a wrap-around skirt by women's dance groups.

Above: "Nake and his bride", c.1900s, Solomon Islands. Probably photographed at New Georgia or Vella Lavella, dressed in their wedding finery of shell valuables, both Nake and his wife are wearing breechclouts of plain tapa fitted as appropriate for a man and a woman. At the rear, the woman's would have been padded out over her bottom.

Left: Tapa, Roviana district, New Georgia Island, Solomon Islands. The men of Roviana wore undecorated breechclouts of white, blue-dyed or naturally red-brown tapa. 199 x 43 cm.

Opposite: Tapa, probably Santa Isabel Island, Solomon Islands. Tapa from the Solomon Islands is sometimes painted with distinctive bold patterns in blue. They are often abstract but sometimes appear to represent human figures or sea creatures such as sharks, fish and dugong. 190 x 121 cm.

The Polynesian people of Rennell and Bellona Islands further to the south continued to wear their undecorated tapa clothing until recently and the methods of manufacture are still well understood. Their dancers frequently appear at festivals, in the Solomons and elsewhere, the men wearing traditional breechclouts of white tapa and headcloths stained bright orange with turmeric.

Throughout the rest of the Solomons, tapa was made for minor domestic purposes, such as slings to carry babies. In some areas it was used for small items of clothing but in other places clothing was minimal, or considered unnecessary. Costume, therefore, depended on a range of spectacular body ornaments of teeth and shell valuables.

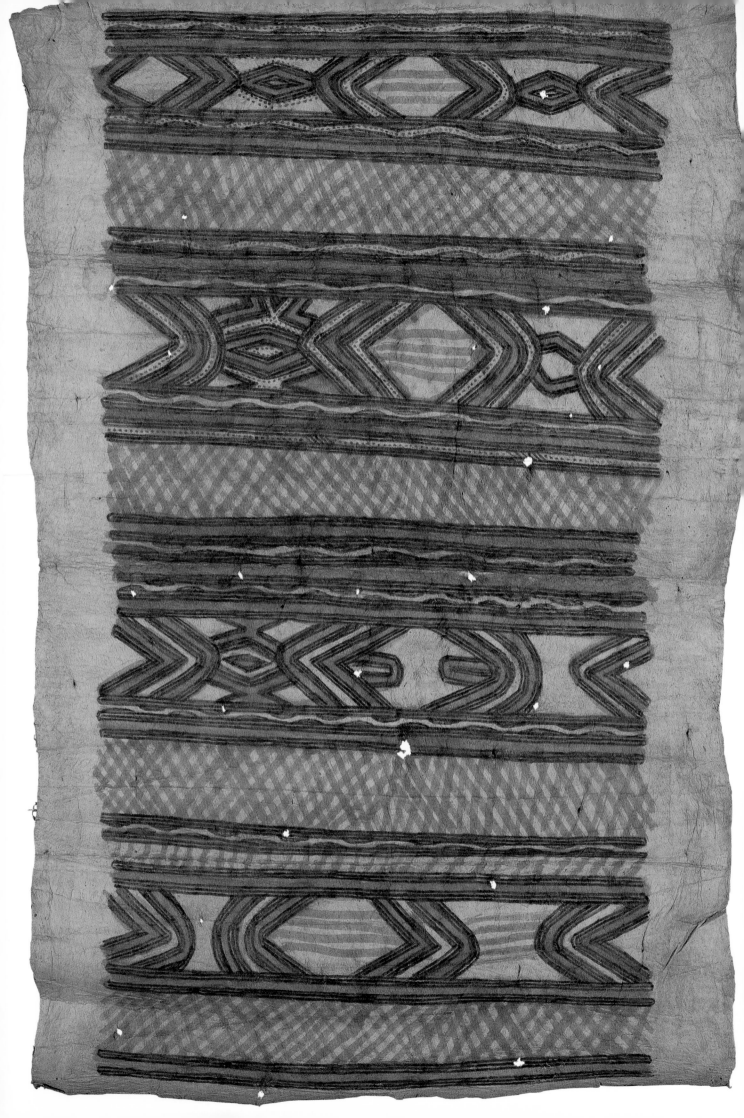

CHAPTER 17

PAPUA NEW GUINEA

The immense cultural diversity of Papua New Guinea is reflected in the diverse tapa-making traditions of this large country. Most are still poorly documented. Speaking approximately seven hundred different languages, the people of Papua New Guinea number about three and a half million, making this the most culturally diverse country in the world. Although their cultures share basic subsistence similarities in horticulture, hunting and fishing, there are significant variations in kinship and social relations, religious rituals, architecture, visual artforms, clothing styles, types of leadership, warfare, trading patterns, and funerary customs. Many of these variations are expressed in the different kinds and different uses of tapa cloth.

Only some of the cultural groups of Papua New Guinea make tapa cloth, and there are few connections between those that do. The prehistory of tapa manufacture goes back so far into the distant past of these islands that the present discontinuous distribution offers no real clues to the initial origin and spread of the complex. Sophisticated horticulture has been practised in the central highland valleys for about nine thousand years, so there has been an immense time-span enabling the tapa-producing plants and techniques to diffuse widely in all directions. Complicating this picture is the wide range of plants used for tapa, many of which have not been identified botanically. Paper mulberry is used in some areas, but various breadfruit, fig and even mangrove species are employed elsewhere. While women usually make the tapa for ordinary clothing as in the rest of the Pacific, a major feature of Papua New Guinea tapa is the prominent role of male craftsmen, especially in the making and decorating of tapa that will be used on ritual occasions as dress-clothing and for masks and figures. And unlike most Pacific tapa beaters which are made of wood, those of Papua New Guinea may also be made of shell (as in the Admiralty Islands and parts of New Britain), or of stone (as in the eastern highlands and Huon Gulf).

In much of Papua New Guinea, tapa is made in smaller pieces and incorporated into various types of objects or shaped to form loincloths or other particular items of dress, rather than being produced in large sheets as in most of Polynesia. Everyday tapa clothing in Papua New Guinea usually consists of breechclouts, loincloths, wrap-around skirts and cloaks. For most of these the tapa cloth is left plain, but some groups decorate the cloth with painted patterns, special fringes, or attached ornaments, such as beads, seeds and feathers. Tapa worn for ritual and ceremonial occasions is almost always decorated, especially the loincloths for men, which may be long soft narrow strips worn as a train, or broad stiff frontlets designed to display their coloured patterns as a complement to other ornaments of shell, teeth and feathers worn by important men. On festive occasions in the Admiralty Islands, brides and other women wore tapa loincloths at back and front, decorated with tassels of seeds, feathers and shell money beads in a display of their family wealth.

One of the best known tapa-producing areas of Papua New Guinea lies in Oro (formerly Northern) Province on the north coast, extending around the shores of Dyke Ackland Bay and Collingwood Bay on both sides of Cape Nelson, inland

Tapa, Oro Province, Papua New Guinea. 121 x 80 cm.

Left: Women beating barkcloth, 1922, Wanigela village, Collingwood Bay, Papua New Guinea. Working outside in the cool of the morning, the bark that these women are beating was reported to be from paper mulberry trees. They both wear barkcloth wrap-around skirts.

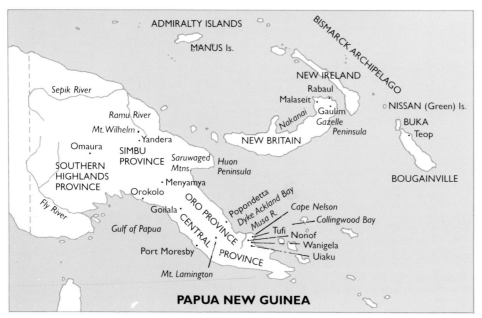

among the Managalase and the Orokaiva on the slopes of Mount Lamington, and among the Binandere who live in coastal swamps to the north. These peoples make colourful bold-patterned tapa in sheets of sizes to suit women's wrap-around *lavalava* and men's loincloths. Larger sheets were formerly made for use as blankets on cooler nights; these also helped to keep the mosquitoes away. Other uses included the covering of cooked food and the wrapping of a body before burial. In these cultures, tapa is an important part of the gifts exchanged at marriage, with the quality and quantity adding to the prestige of giver and receiver.

Among the Orokaiva by the 1950s, tapa clothing had been abandoned for daily wear, with traditional tapa dress being reserved for dances, initiation ceremonies and other special occasions. By the 1960s, people in Wanigela village on the Collingwood Bay coast were no longer wearing tapa cloth in daily life and had ceased making it. But six hours' walking distance south along the coast, at the village of Uiaku, women still preferred tapa cloth to European clothing and were actively making large amounts of tapa. With their bright patterns and convenient sizes, Oro Province tapa has readily translated into a commercial art attractive to collectors and tourists. This new demand has helped to keep the knowledge and skill of tapa-making alive, and in some villages has revived and stimulated increased production.

Loincloth, Huon Peninsula,
Papua New Guinea.
107 × 99 cm.

In the tapa-making villages of Oro Province, paper mulberry trees are cultivated in plantations along the river banks and in plots near the houses. Other wild trees were also used for tapa-making. After beating out the inner bark and drying it in the sun, women paint the designs on freehand with a brush made from tufts of frayed black palm, betel nut husk or pandanus fruit. The favourite colours here are red, from vegetable dyes, and black and brown, from charcoal and certain muds. The designs are first outlined in black and then other colours added later. Finally, the freshly painted tapa sheets are hung out in the sun to dry before being folded and stored in the houses.

Most of these painted patterns appear as abstract and geometric designs, but their names often associate them with plants and animals of the local environment. Specific designs are regarded as the property of different clans and family groups, sometimes because the pattern represents their totemic animal or plant. Clan designs are not normally painted on tapa intended to serve as gifts or trade items. To use these patterns without authority is thought to cause sickness and death among the offending family. However, in recent times, with the development of tapa production for sale to tourists, this copyright system has broken down, especially as women have begun to copy patterns from magazines and other foreign sources.

Above: Widows under barkcloth, 1922, Wanigela village, Collingwood Bay, Papua New Guinea. After a man's death, his wives entered a period of seclusion, hiding under their house and wearing ornaments of Job's Tears seeds and clay body paint as mourning dress. When they needed to leave the house, they had to crawl along hidden under a sheet of barkcloth. They followed a trail marked by another person dragging a stick on the ground. Sheets of barkcloth were laid over the man's grave.

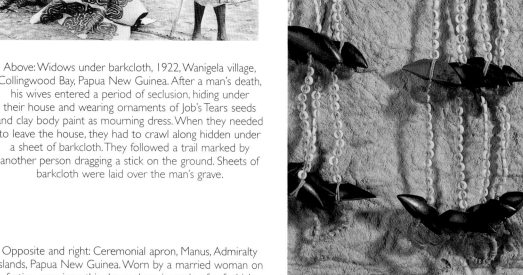

Opposite and right: Ceremonial apron, Manus, Admiralty Islands, Papua New Guinea. Worn by a married woman on festive occasions, this dance dress is made of soft thick barkcloth, decorated with tassels of seeds and shell money beads. A detail is shown right. 98 × 52 cm.

Family groups in the Baruga-speaking villages on the lower Musa River in Dyke Ackland Bay further distinguish their clan and family membership with distinctive fringes cut along the lower edges of their tapa cloth. A person who is able to wear certain fringes by right of family membership can display high social status by the complexity and variety of fringes on his or her tapa clothing.

As in much of Melanesia, many of the cultures of Papua New Guinea are centred on the institutions of men's club houses, secret societies and initiations for young men. The ceremonies and rituals associated with these institutions often require special dress and body decoration, special ritual objects, and masks which represent various spirits. Some Papua New Guinea cultural groups, especially on the coasts and in the nearby islands, are famous for their spectacular masks, which are often made of tapa material, usually supported on a framework of cane, wood or bamboo. The most amazing and largest of these tapa masks, up to 12 metres (40 feet) high, are rarely found in museum collections because they are too large and fragile to collect or were ritually destroyed at the end of the ceremonial cycle. Since most of these ceremonies have now ceased as a result of Western impact, early photographs of these large masks are often the only evidence that has survived, but smaller examples are held in museum collections.

The large island of New Britain in the Bismarck Archipelago was the home of several masking traditions involving the construction of various sorts of tapa masks. Probably the best known of these are the masks of breadfruit tree bark made and worn by the Baining people who live in the mountainous interior of the Gazelle Peninsula at the eastern end of New Britain. A bewildering variety of masks was made by different Baining dialect groups, complicated by different masks used for day and night dances. The day dances served as a mourning ceremony to commemorate

Men dressed for dancing, 1900s, Wanigela village, Collingwood Bay, Papua New Guinea. Wearing new barkcloth loincloths for a dance, these men also display their fighting ornaments. Two on the right have their boars' tusks face ornament now hanging on their chests, but they would be held in their teeth during dance and fighting. Others wear the hornbills' beaks head-dress originally reserved for warriors who had killed an enemy.

those who had died during the previous year and to celebrate the ripening of the taro harvest and other aspects of fertility. It was a ritual activation of a cyclical pattern of birth, growth and death experienced by all living things. The night dances were associated with the initiation of young men into adulthood and as young warriors. Individual masks represent various animals, such as flying foxes, owls, rats, pigs and composite beings such as snake/birds and human/birds, while others are still more abstract. All are emblematic of the spiritual forces that control the human activities of hunting and gathering, warfare and gardening. In the dramatic night dances, masked participants ran through the bonfire that illuminated the scene until just before sunrise when the last dancers stamped out the embers and retreated back into the jungle, leaving a small group of women to dance and celebrate the new day.

Some of the day and night dance ceremonies still continue among the Baining today, featuring masks constructed in the old traditional materials, but decorated with felt-pen designs instead of natural traditional dyes. Other new types of masks and display figures are still being invented and danced in Baining villages as part of the ongoing modern culture of these people. As in the old days, all of these masks are normally used only once and then destroyed or discarded. Those now in museums have been retained by missionaries, administrators and collectors, or made specifically for sale.

Most of the other masking traditions of Papua New Guinea have not survived the impact of European penetration so well. Further west along the north coast of New Britain, a tapa masking tradition of the Nakanai people made one of its last appearances in 1952, in a funerary ritual for an important man at Silanga Mission station. Several of the participants wore tapa masks and capes, and the body was covered by tapa cloth shrouds, all of which were decorated with coloured designs, including some using coloured chalks and commercial oil paints. This particular funeral ceremony was heavily influenced by Christian practices, but it represents an authentic development from an ancient Nakanai tapa tradition and illustrates the continuing important association of tapa with rites of passage and the world of spirits. In a traditional Nakanai funerary ritual, after several months of dancing, feasting and processions, the mourning was concluded when all of the barkcloth costumes were consigned to the grave with the body. This explains why Nakanai tapa is so rare in museum collections.

Among the Tolai neighbours of the Baining, black and white conical bark masks and leaf body covers were worn for funeral ceremonies and ancestor

Tapa mask cover, Nakanai people, New Britain, Papua New Guinea. This mask cover was made in the early 1950s near Silanga Mission station by men of the Vere language group within the Nakanai culture area. It was used for funeral ceremonies which marked the death of an important man. Mounted and sewn on to a light framework of sticks, the mask was worn with a decorated barkcloth cape. 99 x 77 cm.

commemorations by male members of a secret society called *Duk-duk*, which still functions today. Further to the west of New Britain on Buka Island, another little-known men's secret society called *Kokorra* has been compared to the *Duk-duk* of the Tolai. As seen in the later nineteenth century, conical *Kokorra* masks were made of tapa stretched over a frame of bamboo strips and painted with a coloured stylised face on white. Protruding ears were made of wood or tapa-covered cane. Worn by young men dressed in a long brown shirt of tapa which covered the body, they were paraded through the villages to frighten women and children in an act of social control which asserted the power of the men's society.

On the mainland of Papua, the best-known tapa masks are those formerly made by the Elema people of Orokolo Bay, at the head of the Papuan Gulf, for their *Hevehe* ceremonies. Although declining by the 1930s and defunct by the early 1950s, enough

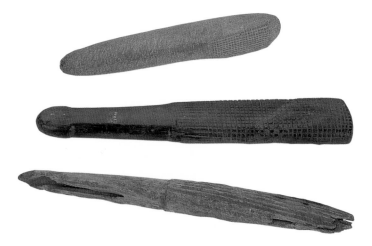

Below: Tapa beaters, Papua New Guinea. Reflecting the great cultural diversity of Papua New Guinea, the names and forms of tapa beaters throughout the country are very varied. To make the beater at the top, the Anga people around Menyamya shaped the stone by hammer-dressing. The grooves were then marked in with a bamboo template. 33 cm long. The middle beater was made of palmwood and called a *kasea* by the people of the Papuan Gulf. 41 cm long. The beater at the bottom was obtained at Omaura village in the Southern Highlands in the 1970s, but it is probably much older than that. 41.3 cm long.

Above: Baining day dancers, 1933, Gazelle Peninsula, New Britain. Wearing *oggeroggeruk* masks, these are probably North-west (Chachet) Baining men, although at this period the Central (Kairak) Baining were making masks like this called *mendas*, which were later adopted by the North-west Baining.

has been recorded and collected to convey the dramatic richness and artistic variety of the *Hevehe* ceremonial cycle. Lasting from ten to twenty years, the cycle involved two main types of barkcloth masks called *hevehe* and *eharo*, carved ancestor boards, decorated bullroarers and other ritual apparatus, all choreographed around the men's long house, which was the focus of village communal life. The *ma-hevehe* are dangerous sea spirits who threaten trading voyages and fishing activities. They visit the village and enter the men's house in the form of *hevehe* masked figures. The creatures wore tapa masks up to 5 metres (16 feet) high in the shape of bullroarers and decorated with painted clan symbols. Young male initiates were introduced to their cult by clan elders while other men, dressed in *eharo* barkcloth masks representing totemic and mythical creatures, danced and enacted comic entertainment around the village. At the dramatic climax and conclusion of the cycle, all of the *hevehe* masks would emerge from the long house and parade through the village to dance on the beach before returning to the long house for the last time. When the cycle was complete, the sacred *hevehe* masks were burnt, but the common *eharo* masks were often kept by their owners, explaining why mostly only *eharo* masks and rarely *hevehe* masks have found their way into museum collections.

Cloak, Anga (Kukukuku) people, Menyamya, Papua New Guinea. Both men
and women among the Anga wear barkcloth cloaks for protection against
rain and cold in the chilly, high, hill country around Menyamya. At night,
their cloaks serve as a mattress and bedcover. Usually made from fig tree bark,
the cloaks of the Anga are always left plain without any painted designs.
This cloak was collected at a village near Menyamya by Seventh Day Adventist
missionaries in the early 1970s. 111 cm long.

Right: Loincloth, Huon Peninsula, Papua New Guinea. 104 × 88 cm.

Below right: Loincloth, Huon Peninsula, Papua New Guinea. 109 × 89 cm.

Opposite: Loincloths, Papua New Guinea. Left: Recorded by Edge-Partington as coming from the Elema people of Orokolo, this freehand decorated loincloth may have originated from one of the groups closer to Port Moresby – perhaps the Mekeo, who wear long narrow loincloths like this as part of their dance costume. 194 × 12 cm. Middle: This cloth was made in Oro Province, perhaps in one of the villages along the shore of Collingwood Bay or around Cape Nelson. 243 × 24 cm. Right: Broader than most loincloths, this one is unfinished and awaiting further painting with red pigment. 228 × 68 cm.

Left: Man's waistband, Yandera, Mount Wilhelm, Papua New Guinea. Made of bark bast with decorative stitching and twisted cords, the narrow frontal cover has been beaten to a definite pattern. 58 cm long.

Opposite: Tapa, Oro Province, Papua New Guinea. Worn by women as wrap-around skirts, sheets of decorated barkcloth are also presented at marriage ceremonies. 143 x 89 cm.

Below: Cloak, Papua New Guinea. This cloak is made from one piece of tapa cloth folded over at the top to take a drawcord and loosely stitched together down the sides to produce a double-layered garment intended for warmth. The freehand design, now much faded, is painted on the outer layer only. Its function as a cloak suggests an origin in one of the higher, colder areas of the country, perhaps inland on the mountainous Huon Peninsula. 116 x 118 cm.

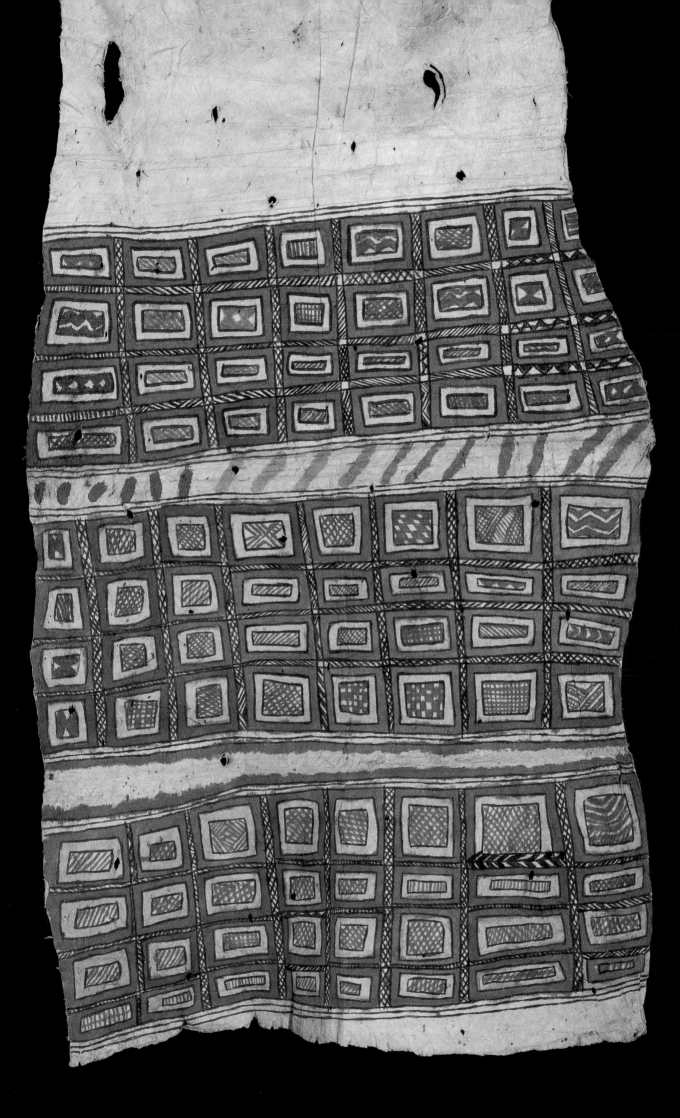

Tapa, Popondetta, Oro Province, Papua New Guinea. 150 x 79 cm.

Tapa, Wanigela, Oro Province, Papua New Guinea. Collected in 1964 in Wanigela, this barkcloth may have been made there by a woman from Uiaku village, where the production of barkcloth was still flourishing at this time. 131 x 67 cm.

Left: Tapa, Oro Province, Papua New Guinea. Made in 1975 by a woman named Airara, this cloth is a good example of the careful neat painting done on modern tapa cloth in this area. 165 x 80 cm.

Following pages: Cape, Nakanai people, New Britain, Papua New Guinea. Made for a funeral ceremony, this cape has been decorated with coloured chalks. It was worn hanging vertically down the back of one of the male participants who carried the deceased. 135 x 75 cm.

Right: Tapa, Oro Province, Papua New Guinea. Made in the 1980s for sale to tourists, this cloth, with its neat painting and standardised measurements, is nevertheless good evidence that the tourist art market can help to sustain the survival of a local indigenous artform. 168 x 86 cm.

1	2	3
4	5	6

1: Mask decoration, Baining people, Malaseit village, Gazelle Peninsula, New Britain, Papua New Guinea. Made in 1966, this shield-shaped barkcloth construction was mounted at the top of an *oggeroggeruk* type of mask worn by a man in a daytime dance at the North-west (Chachet) Baining village of Malaseit. 190 x 67 cm.

2: *Kavat* spirit mask, Baining people, Gaulim village, Gazelle Peninsula, New Britain, Papua New Guinea. Worn by Kairak Baining men of Gaulim village during night dances that last throughout the night and involve the handling of snakes, this *kavat* spirit mask was made and used in 1966. The barkcloth has been stretched and stitched over a bamboo framework. *Kavat* spirits are thought to live in trees in the bush like birds. 68 x 22 cm.

3: *Kokorra* mask, Teop, North Bougainville, Papua New Guinea. Although collected in northern Bougainville, the ceremonies involving this form of mask seem to have been centred on Buka Island and Nissan or Green Island to the north of Bougainville. It was worn with a long brown shirt of tapa. 58 cm high x 39 cm diameter.

4: *Eharo* mask, Elema people, Orokolo Bay, Gulf of Papua, Papua New Guinea. This mask of painted tapa mounted on a cane framework was made by men of the Elema tribe in the large village of Orokolo for a cycle of elaborate masked ceremonies taking ten to twenty years to complete. Various painted designs outlined in split cane stitched on the barkcloth were the property of different clans. 191 x 90 cm.

5: *Eharo* mask, Elema people, Orokolo Bay, Gulf of Papua, Papua New Guinea. As with all the Elema barkcloth masks, a mantle of frayed sago leaves was worn to cover the body of the masked dancer. 74 x 29 cm.

6: *Eharo* mask, Elema people, Orokolo Bay, Gulf of Papua, Papua New Guinea. This mask and mask 4 were collected at Orokolo by F.E. Williams, the Papuan Government's official anthropologist, who made the most intensive study of the *Hevehe* ceremonies just before their final disappearance. 199 x 87 cm.

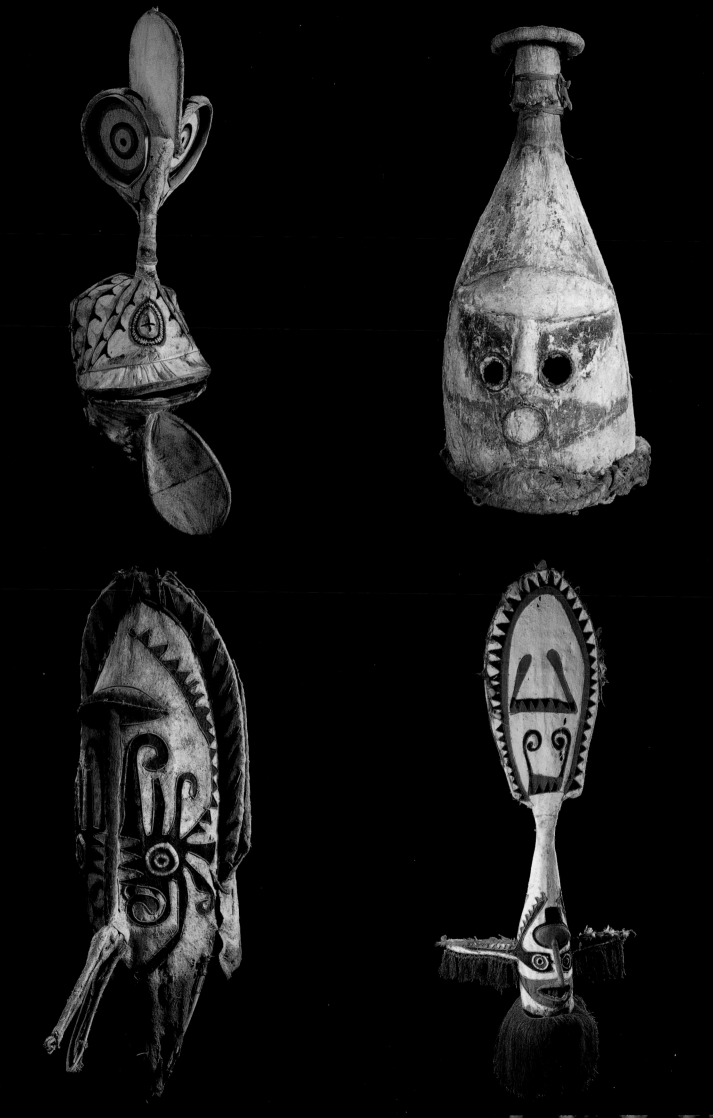

Kavat spirit mask, Baining people, Gazelle Peninsula, New Britain, Papua New Guinea. Among the Central (Kairak) Baining there are many different forms of *kavat* masks, each with a distinctive reference to features of the natural world. This modern example (1990) at left is decorated with felt pens. A rear view of the mask is shown below left and a detail of the pattern is opposite. 147 x 93 cm.

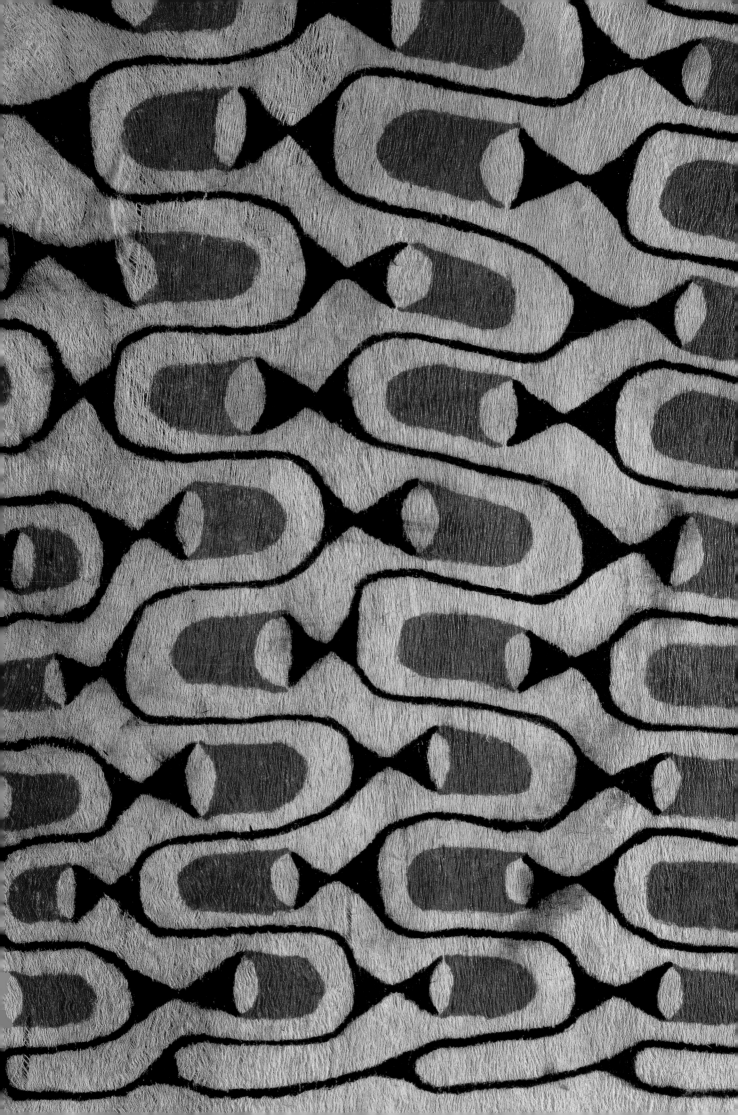

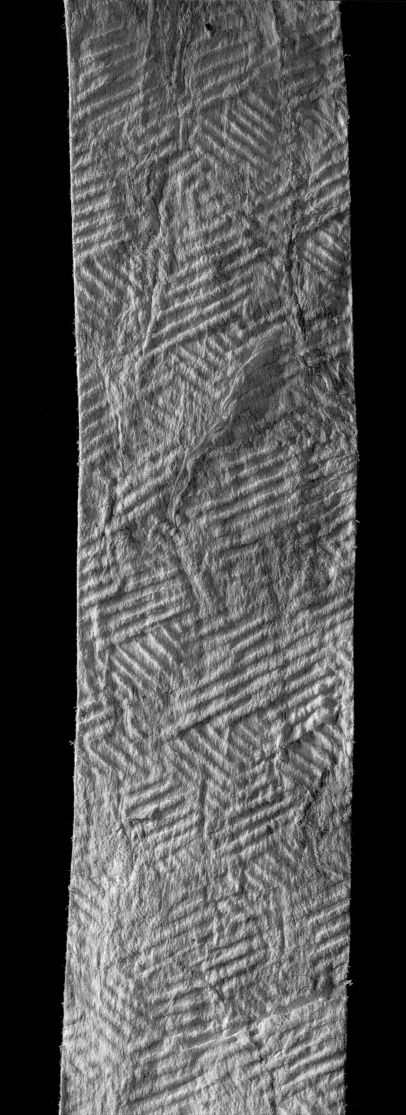

A NOTE ON THE COLLECTIONS

The collection of tapa cloth and associated artefacts now in the Auckland Museum has come from a wide variety of sources, over many years. There are now approximately 400 tapa items in Auckland Museum and further pieces are constantly being added to the collection.

Many have come from interested individuals who have generously presented items to the museum. Their contribution is acknowledged in the Illustrations List by the surname of the donor and the year in which the item was presented to the museum. Other pieces have been purchased either privately, or at auction by the museum for the collection, using museum funds, and these are identified in the Illustrations List by the word "purchased", followed by the year of purchase.

Another important group of tapa pieces in Auckland Museum is from a large collection of Pacific Island artefacts assembled by James Edge-Partington, an English authority on the material culture of the Pacific. He travelled through Australia, New Zealand and the Pacific between 1879 and 1881 and much of his collection was obtained in the course of these travels. After his return to England, he continued to collect Pacific artefacts that became available there. In 1924, his collection of approximately 2500 items was purchased in England by Mrs Selwyn Upton and Mr W. Cecil Leys. They presented it to Auckland Museum in memory of their late father, Dr T.W. Leys, who had a long and distinguished association with Auckland Museum.

As with most museum collections of artefacts, the records of where the item was collected are often vague and unreliable. Even where the locality of collection has been carefully recorded, this does not always mean that the item was made there. This is especially true for such a portable material as tapa cloth, which was traded and exchanged around the islands by the Islanders themselves and by European settlers and travellers. The situation is further complicated by the resettlement of some Pacific island communities in other Pacific island countries where they continued to make barkcloth in their own original style. This uncertainty is sometimes reflected in the captions in this book, where the stated origin may not be the place where the cloth was actually collected, or may be an origin attributed to an unlocalised cloth by the authors on the basis of their knowledge of similar items.

For dates of manufacture, the records are usually even more vague. Obviously, the item must have been made before the recorded date of acquisition by the museum, but in almost all cases that is the only definite date available. Barkcloth does not usually last very long in a village situation but some have been held in private collections for many years before coming to the museum. Except for the few rare early pieces, most of the items illustrated in this book were made at some time between the 1880s and the 1990s.

Opposite: Man's waistband, Aneityum, Vanuatu.
This long narrow piece of tapa, intended to pass
around the man's waist several times, has been
left uncoloured but an indented pattern has been
produced by careful beating. 251 x 6 cm.

GLOSSARY

ahufara shawl or scarf of tapa (Tahiti)

anvil beam or platform on which the bast is beaten, usually of wood, stone in some areas

ariki sacred chief (Tikopia)

Arioi society group of young men and women performers and artists who travelled around the islands in the name of the god Oro (Society Islands)

aute barkcloth (New Zealand)

baba type of tapa design roller with medium spaced grooves (Fiji)

bast the inner bark of trees used for making tapa

bitu ni kesakesa wooden or bamboo grooved roller for applying a pattern to tapa (Fiji)

Duk-duk a male secret society (Papua New Guinea)

eharo mask of tapa on a cane frame, worn in the *hevehe* ceremonial cycle (Papua New Guinea)

'ele term for red ochre (Samoa)

'elei process of rubbing tapa on a design tablet (Samoa)

eva mourning ceremonies (Cook Islands)

feta'aki small pieces of beaten tapa cloth that are assembled into full-size sheets (Tonga)

fusi strip of tapa worn as a belt (Samoa)

gatu vakatoga a variety of Fijian tapa with the design imprinted by rubbing on a design tablet (Fiji)

gatu vakaviti a variety of Fijian tapa with the design combining areas rubbed on a design tablet with borders decorated by stencils and freehand painting (Fiji)

Hala Paini design representing the avenue of Norfolk pine trees near the Royal Palace, Nukualofa, Tonga

hevehe large tapa masks used in the *hevehe* ceremonial cycle (Papua New Guinea)

hiapo term for barkcloth (Niue)

holo large sheets of tapa used for bed covers and screens (Uvea)

i'e tapa beater (Samoa, Rurutu)

i'e kuku tapa beater (Hawaii)

'ie toga fine mat, the most important of Samoan valuables

ike tapa beater (Niue, Society Islands, Cook Islands, Tonga, etc.)

kapa term for barkcloth (Hawaii)

kapa moe sleeping coverings of tapa (Hawaii)

kava drink made from the kava plant

kalou tapa motif (Tonga)

Kavat mask of tapa representing bush spirits made by the Baining people (Papua New Guinea)

kie prestigious plaited mat of pandanus (Tikopia)

kihei shoulder cape made of tapa (Hawaii)

Kokorra male secret society and associated masks of tapa (Buka, Nissan and Bougainville Islands)

kupesi design tablet (Tonga)

kuveji design tablet or rubbing board, also called *kupeti* (Fiji)

lafi 1. wrap-around skirt with rubbed pattern (Uvea). 2. paper mulberry plant (Futuna). 3. long narrow strips of white cloth with a black pattern, worn over the shoulders by men (Futuna)

langalanga a unit of measure used to describe the length of a tapa (Tonga)

lavalava wrap-around skirt worn by both men and women

lepau term for barkcloth (Santa Cruz)

lewasanga type of tapa design roller with fine narrow grooves (Fiji)

liku Fijian woman's fringed skirt of plant fibre

ma-hevehe sea spirits (Papua New Guinea)

malo long narrow garment worn by men, passing between the legs and concealing the genitals (Hawaii, Fiji))

manaia leader of the young men of a Samoan village

manulua tapa motif (Tonga)

maro loincloth of tapa worn by men (Tahiti)

maro aute aprons or girdles made of barkcloth (New Zealand)

maro tafi tapa stained with turmeric (Tikopia)

maro tea white tapa (Tikopia)

masi tapa (Fiji)

masi bolabola tapa made in Cakaudrove district with motifs said to be similar to patterns formed in plaiting coconut leaves (Fiji)

masi kesa Fijian tapa decorated with stencil patterns

masi kuvui tapa coloured by smoking (Fiji)

masi vakadrau variety of *masi vulavula* in which the joins hang free to form fringes (Fiji)

masi vulavula white tapa (Fiji)

matai elected holder of a traditional title (Samoa)

meke dance (Fiji)

mendas type of barkcloth mask made by the Central Baining people (Papua New Guinea)

mo'u grass fibres used as paint brushes (Tahiti)

ngatu tapa (Tonga, Uvea)

ngatu'uli dark tapa exchanged at weddings (Tonga)

nemasitse barkcloth (Eromanga, Vanuatu)

nifo'oti type of wooden club and later metal weapon (Samoa)

noa type of tapa design roller with alternating wide and narrow grooves (Fiji)

oggeroggeruk type of tapa mask made by the North-west Baining people (Papua New Guinea)

pa fortified village (New Zealand)

paoi pounder or tapa beater (New Zealand)

pare eva, pare tareka masks covered with barkcloth (Cook Islands)

pareu woman's garment of tapa worn around the waist (Tahiti)

pau 1. wild indigo, used for colouring tapa (New Georgia and Santa Isabel, Solomon Islands). 2. woman's garment of tapa worn around the waist (Tahiti)

pa'u woman's wrap-around skirt (Hawaii)

pupuni tapa curtain for dividing a room (Samoa)

raroa woman's wrap-around skirt (Tikopia)

salatasi a waist garment with extremely fine black patterns (Futuna)

siapo tapa (Samoa, Futuna)

siapo 'elei tapa patterned from a design tablet, also called *siapo tasina* (Samoa)

siapo mamanu freehand painted tapa (Samoa)

siapo tasina tapa patterned from a design tablet, also called *siapo 'elei* (Samoa)

siapo vala piece of tapa worn by orator (Samoa)

Sila o Tonga the royal seal of Tonga

sisi necklace of whales' teeth (Fiji)

sua ta'i formal presentation of gifts to honoured guests (Samoa)

ta'alolo gift procession (Samoa)

tabua whale's tooth presented as ceremonial gift (Fiji)

ta'i namu mosquito curtain (Samoa)

tapa the undecorated strip along each side of a tapa (Tonga, Samoa)

tapa'ingatu tapa decorated by rubbing only over the actual design tablets, leaving the surrounding cloth white (Tonga)

taunamu mosquito curtain (Fiji)

taupou village virgin, the leader of the young women (Samoa)

tepi wrap-around skirt worn by men for dancing (Futuna)

tikoru thick white tapa made by men, used in ritual (Mangaia, Cook islands)

tiputa Polynesian poncho made from tapa

tohihina wrap-around skirt decorated with freehand patterns, including fine black lines (Uvea)

tokelau feletoa decorative motif on tapa (Tonga)

to'oto'o orator's staff (Samoa)

tuiga headdress of *manaia* and *taupou* (Samoa)

tutua wooden anvil on which tapa is beaten (Samoa)

upeti design tablet from which the pattern is transferred to the tapa by rubbing (Samoa)

vane-swastika term coined to describe a tapa motif with windmill-like vanes in a swastika arrangement

BIBLIOGRAPHY

Buck, P., 'Samoan Material Culture', *B. P. Bishop Museum Bulletin* 75, 1930.

Burrows, E. G., 'Ethnology of Futuna', *B. P. Bishop Museum Bulletin* 138, 1936.

Clunie, F., *Yalo i Viti, Shades of Fiji, a Fiji Museum Catalogue*, Suva, Fiji Museum, 1986.

Corbin, G.A., 'The Art of the Baining: New Britain', in Mead, S. M. (Ed.), *Exploring the Visual Art of Oceania*, Honolulu, University Press of Hawaii, 1979.

Cox, P.O. and Banak, S.A. (Eds.), *Islands, Plants and Polynesians, An Introduction to Polynesian Ethnobotany*, Portland, Dioscorides Press, 1991.

Ewins, R., *Fijian Artefacts, Tasmanian Museum and Art Gallery Collection*, Hobart, Tasmanian Museum and Art Gallery, 1982.

Kooijman, S., 'Tapa in Polynesia', *B. P. Bishop Museum Bulletin* 234, 1972.

Kooijman, S., *Tapa on Moce Island, Fiji, A Traditional Handicraft in a Changing Society*, Leiden, Rijksmuseum voor Volkenkunde, 1977.

Kooijman, S., *Polynesian Barkcloth*, Aylesbury, Shire Ethnography, 1988.

Leonard, A. and Terrell, J., *Patterns of Paradise*, Chicago, Field Museum of Natural History, 1980.

Mosuwadoga, G. N., *Traditional Techniques and Values in the Lower Musa River*, Waigani, Papua New Guinea National Museum and Art Gallery, 1977.

Neich, R., 'Material Culture of Western Samoa: Persistence and Change', *National Museum of New Zealand Bulletin* 23, 1985.

Neich, R., 'New Zealand Maori Barkcloth and Barkcloth Beaters', *Records of the Auckland Institute and Museum* 33, 1996.

Pritchard, M., *Siapo: Bark Cloth Art of Samoa*, American Samoa Council on Culture, Arts and Humanities, 1984.

Schwimmer, Z., 'Tapa Cloths of the Northern District, Papua New Guinea', *Pacific Arts Newsletter* 9, 1979.

Tiesler, F., 'Tapa aus der Collingwood Bay', *Kleine Beitrage aus dem Staatlichen Museum fur Volkerkunde Dresden* 13, 1993.

Williams, F.E., *Drama of Orokolo*, Oxford, Oxford University Press, 1940.

ILLUSTRATION LIST

The following illustration list gives a brief caption title, size of the tapa, registration number and date of purchase or presentation to the Auckland Museum (if applicable). All photographs are by Krzysztof Pfeiffer, Auckland Museum, unless otherwise stated. The illustrations, both colour and black and white, are in order of appearance in the book, the first number being the page number. Abbreviations: AM, Auckland Museum, ATL, Alexander Turnbull Library Wellington; ML, Mitchell Library, State Library of New South Wales, Sydney; MONZ, Museum of New Zealand, Wellington

1 Motif, Tonga
2 *Siapo tasina*, 241 × 180 cm, AM 54208
3 Tapa mask cover, 41 × 31 cm, AM 55160, purchased 1996
4 Motif, Tonga, [reg. no.]
6-7 *Siapo mamanu*, 184 × 143 cm, AM 4336, presented Kay, 1929
8 Map, Pacific Islands
10 Paper mulberry tree, photo: Roger Neich
11 Samoan girl in studio, photo: Thomas Andrew, MONZ, C 1454
12 Tapa manufacture, photos: Roger Neich, MONZ, CT 3679, 3682, 3697, 3685, 3693, 3699, 3708
14 *Toto'a* overpainting the imprinted design, photo: Roger Neich
15 above, Designs carved on both sides of the *upeti*, photo: Roger Neich; below, Two *siapo vala*, photos: Roger Neich
17 A selection of *siapo vala*, photos: Roger

Neich
18 *Siapo mamanu*, 208 × 167 cm, AM 8481, presented Mitchelson, 1920
19 Orator chiefs, photo: ATL, F 116319 1/2
20 above, left, Orator chief and family, photo: Museum für Völkerkunde, Berlin-Dahlem, Germany; above, right, Young men dressed as *manaia*, photo: A.J. Tattersall, Album 2, p. 27, ML; left, Young women in tapa dresses, photo: A.J. Tattersall, Album 3, p.22, ML
21 *Siapo mamanu*, 231 × 186 cm, AM 1800.1, deposited by the Officers' Club, 1927
22 left, *Siapo mamanu*, 218 × 182 cm, AM 30085, presented Aris, 1948; below, Warrior with rifle, photo: Swain and Liddy, Tyrrell Collection, Powerhouse Museum, Sydney
23 *Siapo mamanu*, 160 × 146 cm, Edge-Partington Collection/Leys Memorial, AM 4142.4, presented 1924
24 above, *Siapo mamanu*, 174 × 132 cm,

AM 9602, presented Cresser 1923; below, Young woman dressed as a *taupou*, photo: A.J. Tattersall, Album 2, p.26, ML
25 above, *Siapo mamanu*, 230 × 199 cm, AM 55180; below, Tapa displayed, photo: ATL, F 56039 1/2
26-7 Samoan tapa decorative motifs
28 above, *Siapo mamanu*, 150 × 118 cm, AM 49859.2, presented Hankins, 1982; below, *Siapo mamanu*, 200 × 179 cm, Edge-Partington Collection/Leys Memorial, AM 4135, presented 1924
29 *Siapo mamanu*, 255 × 196 cm, AM 30086, presented Aris, 1948
30 above, *Siapo mamanu*, left, 299 × 32 cm, AM 50828, presented Copeland, 1984; middle, 460 × 50 cm, 21925.4, presented McMillan, 1935; right, 635 × 75 cm, AM 11734, presented Steel, 1886; below, *Siapo mamanu*, 155 cm diameter, Edge-

INDEX